D1604986

DUKE ELLINGTON

DUKE ELLINGTON

SCOTT YANOW

FOREWORD BY DR. BILLY TAYLOR

FRIEDMAN/FAIRFAX
PUBLISHERS

A FRIEDMAN/FAIRFAX BOOK

© 1999 by Michael Friedman Publishing Group, Inc.

All rights reserved. No part of this publication may
be reproduced, stored in a retrieval system, or trans-
mitted, in any form or by any means, electronic,
mechanical, photocopying, recording, or otherwise,
without prior written permission from the publisher.

Library of Congress Cataloging-in-Publication data
available upon request.

ISBN 1-56799-855-0

Editor: Reka Simonsen
Art Director: Jeff Batzli
Designer: Lori Thorn
Photography Editor: Jennifer Bove
Production Manager: Ingrid Neimanis-McNamara

Color separations by Fine Arts Repro House
Printed in Singapore by KHL Printing Co Pte Ltd

10 9 8 7 6 5 4 3 2 1

For bulk purchases and special sales, please contact:
Friedman/Fairfax Publishers
Attention: Sales Department
15 West 26th Street
New York, New York 10010
212/685-6610   FAX 212/685-1307

Visit our website:
http://www.metrobooks.com

FOR MY WIFE, KATHY, AND MY DAUGHTER, MELODY.

CONTE

FOREWORD

DR. BILLY TAYLOR ON DUKE ELLINGTON

My relationship with Duke Ellington was a very personal one. He was quite generous to me. The first time I met him in the mid-1940s, Ben Webster introduced us at the Hurricane Club, and that very night, Duke had me sit in with the band. Whenever he would come to see me at the Hickory House or the other places where I played, he was always very encouraging, as he was to many younger musicians.

One of the most remarkable things that Duke Ellington did in his earlier days was to adapt his music to the three-minute form, saying what he had to say with such brevity that it could fit onto a 78 record and be a complete statement. With "Solitude," "It Don't Mean a Thing (If It Ain't Got That Swing)," "In a Sentimental Mood," "Prelude to a Kiss," and countless other songs that he composed, he really touched people.

Many of us think of the band as Duke Ellington's main instrument, but I have had occasion during the past year, while listening to many of his records, to remember what an astounding pianist he was. His introductions and setups for his soloists were perfectly organized gems. One of the things that Duke and Mary Lou Williams shared and passed on to Thelonious Monk, Randy Weston, and many other people, including myself, was the tradition of playing stride piano and of mastering the instrument with both hands.

As an arranger, Duke had ideas that were quite unusual for his time. Instead of writing a basic part for all the saxophones or all the brass, he would mix up the instruments. He would want to hear different colors, so he would have a muted trombone placed in the middle of the reeds, or a saxophone in the brass section. Yet, no matter how unusual or original his voicings were, they never sounded out of place.

Duke Ellington brought an elegance to jazz that set the standard for others to follow. The guys in his band always looked magical onstage, the lighting was carefully thought out, and his presentation was superb. Duke realized that people saw—as well as listened to—his artists. His legacy, in addition to his presentation, was the refined sound of his music. He could transform a blues song in such a way that one would never realize it was the blues—his renditions had so many beautiful qualities that one would not normally associate with that genre of music. He made it possible for many musicians who do not think of melancholy, sentimental, and thoughtful pieces as means of personal expression to rethink that belief because the ballads he wrote came from so many different points of view.

Every aspect of music that Duke Ellington touched, he made a little bit better.

Dr. Billy Taylor

Dr. Billy Taylor, world-renowned jazz pianist, composer, author, and educator, has been instrumental in keeping Duke Ellington's legacy alive.

INTRODUCTION

THE LIFE OF A GENIUS

I n the history of American music, Duke Ellington stands alone. During a career that spanned nearly half a century he wrote more than a thousand compositions, toured the world with his orchestra ceaselessly, and became one of the most influential jazz musicians ever. More than two decades after his death in 1974, his presence is still felt.

Ellington's songs are played constantly by musicians and singers of all styles; previously unheard studio and live recordings by his big band are discovered and released on a regular basis; New York's Lincoln Center Jazz Orchestra (under the direction of Wynton Marsalis) performs all-Ellington shows; Duke's arranging techniques are studied in music schools; pianists knowingly and sometimes unwittingly "borrow" chords from his unusual playing style—Duke Ellington remains a household name. With the exceptions of Louis Armstrong and Bing Crosby, no other musical performer who matured in the 1920s is as well known to the general public today. That Ellington was able to gain fame and a certain amount of fortune without compromising his art—and by following his own musical path for decades—is remarkable. Music scholars who had previously appreciated only classical music were calling him a genius by the early 1930s; forty years later he was still a modern and creative force, in addition to being a popular performer.

OPPOSITE: Edward Kennedy Ellington's natural elegance earned him the nickname "Duke" when he was still in his teens. Here he looks well dressed, enthusiastic, and ready to embark upon another musical adventure. **ABOVE:** By 1932, Duke Ellington's orchestra was already the most popular in the country. The orchestra is seen here at the Oriental Theatre in Chicago—Duke is leaning on Sonny Greer's kettle drum.

Ellington's energy and involvement in his music never let up. In his late sixties, after leading his band for more than four decades, he still had "that swing."

Most of America's top musical performers have been specialists: their accomplishments have been in just one or two major areas. Al Jolson, Bing Crosby, Frank Sinatra, and Elvis Presley were highly influential singers who also acted now and then. Louis Armstrong, who taught the world how to swing, was equally skilled as a trumpeter and vocalist. George Gershwin was a brilliant composer who also played pretty fair piano while his contemporaries mostly stuck to creating new tunes. Count Basie was quite significant as both a pianist and as a bandleader. Benny Goodman was the world's top clarinetist. John Coltrane was an incredible saxophonist and trumpeter. Bebop founders altoist Charlie Parker and trumpeter Dizzy Gillespie were innovative musicians and composers both. Miles Davis initiated several eras of music with his trumpet playing and ability to recognize young talent.

Duke Ellington and Billy Strayhorn, his closest musical friend and constant collaborator, tinkle the ivories together. Strayhorn gave him his theme song, "Take the 'A' Train."

Duke Ellington, unlike any of these giants, excelled in several areas of music simultaneously. During a nearly fifty-year period, Ellington was at the top of his field in at least four different roles: composer, arranger, pianist, and bandleader. If he had stuck to just one of these fields, and for only two decades instead of five, he would still be remembered today as a major artist.

The sheer quantity of music that Duke Ellington composed is almost unbelievable. He wrote literally thousands of pieces that ranged from conventional songs and moody instrumental sketches to lengthy works. Hundreds of his melodies became standards, and the world would be a lot poorer without such songs as "Mood Indigo," "Sophisticated Lady," "I Got It Bad and That Ain't Good," "Rockin' in Rhythm," "It Don't Mean a Thing (If It Ain't Got That Swing)," "In a Sentimental Mood," "Do Nothing Till You Hear From Me," "Solitude," and "Satin Doll." Unlike his fellow composers Gershwin, Cole Porter, and Irving Berlin, Ellington was constantly on the road running a band (with its many distractions), which makes his prolific writing even more remarkable.

Although Ellington's first love was the piano, he always thought of his orchestra as his main instrument, and his favorite composition was always his next one.

As an arranger, Duke Ellington never adhered to set rules—instead he made up his own approach as he went along. Although he was well aware of Don Redman's innovations from Fletcher Henderson's orchestra in the 1920s (dividing a big band up into trumpet, trombone, and reed sections), Duke preferred to utilize unusual tonal colors and to write around the strengths and weaknesses of individual musicians, combining unlikely players who ranged from virtuosos to primitives. For example, his band in 1932 consisted of trumpeters Cootie Williams (brilliant with mutes), Arthur Whetsol (who had a quiet and thoughtful sound), and Freddy Jenkins (influenced by Louis Armstrong); trombonists Joe "Tricky Sam" Nanton (capable of playing all kinds of bizarre sounds) and the very fluent Lawrence Brown; valve trombonist Juan Tizol (who had brilliant technique); New Orleans clarinetist Barney Bigard; the pacesetting altoist Johnny Hodges, the old-fashioned sounding sweet alto of Otto Hardwick, and baritonist Harry Carney; and a tight rhythm section. It is a testament to Ellington's arranging talents that he could not only get all of these individualists to somehow blend together to form a coherent ensemble but that he could provide them with a showcase better suited to their talents than they could possibly find elsewhere. Few of Duke's sidemen, particularly from the early days, sounded as good outside the world of Ellington as they did during their period with his big band—no wonder many of them stayed for decades.

Duke Ellington thrived on contrasts and individuality. The result was that his music was much more personal than that heard from the usual big band, and nearly impossible to duplicate without having the services of the same musicians. In addition, Ellington frequently rearranged pieces over time, depending on which musicians were available. With "Mood Indigo" (composed in 1930) he originally created a haunting sound by harmonizing trumpet, trombone (played high), and low-register clarinet. In later years the ensemble was altered and the song was reworked using trombone, clarinet, and bass clarinet (in the trumpet's spot), yet it retained its original flavor.

Equally comfortable with people from all walks of life, Duke Ellington performed for several presidents. In 1950, Ellington gave President Harry Truman the original score to a piece that famed conductor Arturo Toscanini had commissioned Ellington to write, "Portrait of New York Suite."

Duke Ellington's first inspirations for playing piano were the many stride players who toured through his native Washington, D.C., as he was growing up, such as the masterful James P. Johnson (whose piano rolls Ellington used to slow down so as to learn to duplicate) and Willie "The Lion" Smith, a veteran pianist who befriended him. But unlike nearly all of the piano players of the 1920s, Duke constantly kept his style modern. Rather than continuing to stride back and forth with his left hand—a carryover from when pianists were often hired as one-man bands to entertain dancers—Ellington always stayed contemporary, switching to a more irregular percussive approach in later years that would be an inspiration for such modern players as Thelonious Monk and the avant-gardist Cecil Taylor. In fact, listening to *Money Jungle*, an Ellington trio record from the early 1960s with bassist Charles Mingus and drummer

Ellington received eleven Grammy awards in the course of his career, including two in 1968, one for Best Instrumental Jazz Performance, Large Group for *...And His Mother Called Him Bill*, and a special Lifetime Achievement award.

ABOVE: Duke Ellington was so impressed by Great Britain's Queen Elizabeth when he met her in 1958 that the following year he and Billy Strayhorn composed and recorded "The Queen's Suite" and sent her the only copy. It was finally released to the public posthumously in 1976. **OPPOSITE:** Ellington did some of his finest writing late at night, after his band had finished performing and the club or concert hall was empty.

Max Roach, one could be excused for believing that the pianist was in his twenties rather than his sixties.

Duke Ellington was virtually the only big-band leader from the swing era (which he actually preceded by a decade) to keep his orchestra together nonstop into the 1970s. From 1926 to 1974, Duke's band always ranked among the top five. Despite difficulties—such as the racism of the era, several changes in the public's musical tastes, close competition, and occasional defections by key sidemen—the Duke Ellington orchestra was a constant for nearly fifty years. It always maintained its musical integrity during a seemingly infinite number of recordings (Duke constantly documented his band in the studios) and live performances.

There is simply no way to explain Duke Ellington's genius. He was mostly self-taught as a pianist, arranger, and composer and, although always quite aware of current musical trends, he stood apart from them, borrowing whatever aspects fit his music and not bothering with faddish and lightweight trappings. He hated to be confined to any specific category, preferring the freedom to constantly grow and change, and therefore disavowed the word "jazz." He claimed that there were only two types of music—good and bad—and considered his favorite artists "beyond category."

Even with the great amount of interest still centered on Duke Ellington, he remains a bit of a mystery figure. He managed to be a public performer whose life was always quite private, a quiet yet outgoing personality who had relatively few close friends, and a very active and charming ladies' man who remained married to his wife despite their permanent separation in 1928. Relaxed, calm, cool, and friendly, Duke Ellington was a person who generally got what he wanted without appearing to ask for it, and one who accomplished a great deal without ever seeming to have worked very hard. He was a truly remarkable man.

THE WASHINGTONIAN

CHAPTER 1

Even at twenty-two, Duke Ellington looked distinguished and mature, as in this 1921 photo taken at the Louis Thomas Cabaret in Washington, D.C. Pictured with him are (left to right) drummer Sonny Greer, singers Bertha Ricks and Mrs. Conaway, and banjoist Sterling Conaway.

From the beginning of his life, Edward Kennedy Ellington had class. His manners were impeccable, he wore tasteful up-to-date clothes, and he delighted in colorful phrases and witty words. His lifelong nickname "Duke" came about because of his superior yet accessible manner, as if he were somehow above it all and apart from the world, yet never snobbish or forbidding.

Duke Ellington was born April 29, 1899, in Washington, D.C., to a middle-class African-American family. His father, James Edward Ellington, was a butler for wealthy white families and in the 1920s worked as a blueprint maker. Duke had very close relationships with his mother, Daisy, and his younger sister, Ruth (who was born in 1915), and was surrounded by music while growing up. The family owned a piano; J.E. played popular songs by ear while Daisy read music and often performed hymns, ballads, and occasionally, ragtime. Being part of a close and loving family helped shield young Duke from the racial tensions of the times, and he had a happy and fairly comfortable childhood.

Ellington took his first formal music lessons when he was seven, from a teacher whose name, remarkably, was Marietta Clinkscales. However, Duke

This 1903 photo finds four-year-old Edward Kennedy Ellington (who was happily spoiled by his mother) looking as if he is eagerly contemplating the future.

managed to miss many of the sessions, and a serious interest in playing music would not develop for a few more years. Around 1913, Ellington began hanging around pool halls, not to hustle or gamble but to socialize with a wide variety of personalities and to hear the local pianists trying to top each other. Duke was very attracted to the glamorous life that musicians seemed to have, and he began to learn tricks on the piano from the older players. Within three years he was talented enough to be playing professionally himself.

Because he was not yet proficient at reading music, Ellington learned mostly by ear. His lack of formal training prevented him from utilizing the conventional ways of solving various musical problems, so he found his own solutions, with the result that he began to develop an original style from his earliest days as a musician. In later years, Ellington would name many of the Washington, D.C., ragtime pianists as inspirations, including Doc Perry, Louis Brown, Louis Thomas, Lester Dishman, Sticky Mack, Clarence Bowser, and Blind Johnny. Unfortunately, none of these men ever made recordings.

In 1914, Duke Ellington composed his first piece, "Soda Fountain Rag," also known as "Poodle Dog Rag" (after the Poodle Dog Café, where Duke had a summer job as a soda jerk and occasionally played piano); his second was the suggestive "What You Going to Do When the Bed Breaks Down?" In addition to playing at the Poodle Dog, other early jobs for the up-and-coming pianist included performing at parties and dances and sitting in at jam sessions. Doc Perry was an important teacher of his during this time, working with Ellington on reading music and chords and now and then using him as a relief pianist.

However, for a period it seemed that Ellington's future career would be in visual art, not in music. He won first prize in a poster contest sponsored by the NAACP, and as a senior at Armstrong High School, Duke was offered an art scholarship to Brooklyn's Pratt Institute. But Ellington eventually decided to stick to music—he was just beginning to make money as a pianist and it looked to be a more lucrative profession.

ABOVE, LEFT: Duke's father, James Edward Ellington (right), is pictured with Billy Butler, a family friend, in Washington, D.C., during the 1920s. Duke greatly admired his father, who combined dignity with a fun-loving nature. **ABOVE, RIGHT:** The death in 1935 of Duke Ellington's beloved mother, Daisy, inspired her son to write the lengthy and brooding "Reminiscing in Tempo." He wanted nothing more in life than to please her, and he succeeded.

Sixteen years younger than Duke, Ruth Ellington was adored by her older and often overprotective brother, who made sure that she always had the best of everything.

With the outbreak of World War I and the influx of government visitors in Washington, young Ellington found many opportunities for work. During the day he made signs and posters (often for dances); at night he played with many local groups and proved to be expert at quickly putting together bands of his own for jobs. He soon formed the Duke's Serenaders, a group whose size and personnel varied according to the engagement itself. Among the sidemen whom Ellington frequently used in the early 1920s were C-melody saxophonist Otto Hardwick (who would later switch to alto), the very lyrical trumpeter Arthur Whetsol, the experienced and colorful drummer Sonny Greer, and banjoist Elmer Snowden; all would play important roles in Duke's band when he eventually moved to New York.

In 1918, Duke Ellington married Edna Thompson and on March 11, 1919, their only child, Mercer Ellington, was born. Duke's musical activities gradually increased

Mercer Ellington, Duke's son, followed in his talented father's footsteps. He played saxophone and trumpet, was an arranger for the orchestra from time to time, and composed some of the orchestra's hit songs, including "Things Ain't What They Used to Be."

during this era. By taking out a large ad in the classified pages of the telephone directory, Ellington was able to get more jobs than he could handle, and his charming personality and showmanship made him quite popular. However, his flashy stage manner was way ahead of his musicianship, a deficiency that Duke was aware of, so he took some needed lessons in fundamentals, harmony, and music reading from Henry Grant, a top local musician.

Between his sign painting and nighttime jobs, Duke was making a good living. He performed at society parties, balls, dances, cabarets, and restaurants. The diverse musical experiences gave Ellington an opportunity to play and relate to a wide variety of audiences in many different circumstances.

By 1923, Ellington was enticed by the glamour of New York, the northern adventures of Sonny Greer and Elmer Snowden, and the desire to make it in a more competitive environment. Wilbur Sweatman, who a decade earlier had been billed as "The Musical Marvel of the Twentieth Century" because he was able to play three clarinets at once (a feat he unfortunately never documented on record), needed a drummer and sent for Greer. Sonny agreed to accept the job if his buddies Ellington and Hardwick were also hired. Sweatman went along with the idea and, although Duke was a bit reluctant to leave his thriving band business, he went up north.

The three Washington musicians performed as part of Sweatman's septet in a vaudeville show during a run at the Lafayette Theatre and for a few other short-term jobs. When Sweatman left town to go on the vaudeville circuit, they decided to stay in town and see what they could find for themselves. Because Greer was a colorful character with a lot of friends, the trio was able to survive for a few months, during which time they met a lot of local musicians, including Willie "The

The Duke Ellington reed section of the 1930s consisted of Otto Hardwick (with Ellington from 1920–28 and 1932–43), Harry Carney (1927–74), Barney Bigard (1927–42), and Johnny Hodges (1928–51 and 1955–70). Collectively they played with Ellington's orchestra for 119 years!

Lion" Smith, who became a lifelong friend and admirer of Ellington. However, money grew quite scarce and eating became an occasional luxury. After they were lucky enough to find fifteen dollars on the street, a disappointed Ellington, Greer, and Hardwick returned home to Washington, D.C.

LEFT: The Wilbur Sweatman Orchestra performed at the Lafayette Theatre in March 1923. From left to right: banjoist Maceo Jefferson, bassist Bob Escudero, Ellington, Sweatman (notice his three clarinets, which he sometimes played at the same time!), drummer Sonny Greer, trombonist John Anderson, and altoist Otto Hardwick. **ABOVE:** The great stride pianist Willie Smith in the 1940s. "The Lion" was a major influence on Ellington's piano style and a lifelong friend. His trademark bowler hat and cigar contrasted with his surprisingly sensitive and sophisticated piano playing.

THE JUNGLE BAND

CHAPTER 2

Duke Ellington's Cotton Club Orchestra of 1931. Altoist Johnny Hodges (on the far left) wears his typical look of boredom, but his deadpan demeanor always hid a romantic soul.

Within a couple of months, a new opportunity arose that allowed Duke Ellington to return to New York. Dancer Clarence Robinson was working with Liza and Her Shuffling Sextet, a vaudeville act that included the great pianist Fats Waller. When they arrived in Washington, D.C., a dispute resulted in the band breaking up. Robinson saw Snowden leading a band that included Ellington, Hardwick, Whetsol, and Greer, and he decided to form a new group. Robinson hired all of the players except Ellington (since he still had Waller) and took them to New York, where he had six weeks of engagements lined up. But the promoters wanted the original band, so all of the work was quickly canceled. Waller soon found another engagement and Snowden, now in need of a pianist, sent for Ellington. When Duke arrived, having spent most of his money on the train ride north, he was dismayed to find that there was no actual work for the players.

Although still struggling, Ellington (then the leader of the Kentucky Club Orchestra) was on the verge of a major breakthrough in 1926, when this photo was taken.

This time the musicians stuck it out. Finally in August, future nightclub owner Ada "Bricktop" Smith found employment for the group at Barron Wilkins' Exclusive Club. The establishment was one of the main hangouts for the elite in Harlem, so wages and tips were quite good for the time, but the musicians had to play each night from 11:00 P.M. until 10:00 A.M. the next day. However, the long hours gave the players an opportunity to develop their own sounds. The music they performed at the Exclusive Club was played sweetly and at a low volume but with inner heat.

In the summer of 1923, Duke Ellington met singer-lyricist Jo Trent and they collaborated on some compositions that they were able to sell to Tin Pan Alley publishers; none became a hit and all are forgotten today, but Ellington now had an excuse to work on his writing skills. One of the publishers who purchased some of Ellington's songs was Irving Mills, who in a few years would become an important force in Duke's life.

In September 1923, Elmer Snowden and his Black Sox Orchestra landed a six-month gig at the Hollywood Club in New York. They changed the name of the band to the Washingtonians, and the group increased to seven pieces with Snowden,

Ellington, Hardwick, and Greer being joined by trombonist John Anderson and Roland Smith on reeds. Most importantly, Arthur Whetsol departed to return to school in Washington and was replaced by cornetist Bubber Miley. The arrival of Miley, a master at using mutes on his horn and creating a wide assortment of unusual growls and cries, was really the birth of the grittier "Jungle Band" sound. When Charlie Irvis (a superior blues player) replaced Anderson early in 1924, the style of the ensemble was completely transformed from sweet to hot, from background dance music to heated and emotional jazz. And when a dispute over money resulted in Snowden being kicked out of the group in February, Duke Ellington became the leader of the Washingtonians.

Ellington's late 1920s orchestra was often known as "The Jungle Band" because of its wild and emotional sounds, which some thought came straight from Africa. Duke's image belied this name, of course—he was always the epitome of worldly sophistication.

Ellington and his longtime banjoist and rhythm guitarist Fred Guy were associated from the beginning of Duke's bandleading days, when Guy replaced Elmer Snowden in 1924. Although his prominence diminished through the years, Guy (seen here in 1926) remained with Ellington until he chose to retire in 1949; he was never replaced.

Although the band had recorded three songs previously under Snowden's name, none was ever released. They made their official recording debut in November 1924 (forty-nine years before Ellington's final recording) and the band, with banjoist Fred Guy permanently taking over Snowden's place, sounds quite identifiable on "Choo Choo" and "Rainy Nights." Strangely enough, their next four recording sessions (held from September 1925 through June 1926), which resulted in eight titles, are not that good, utilizing expanded groups (with some substitute players) and weak arrangements. The recording quality is poor and the musicians clearly needed to grow more before being taken seriously.

After a fire closed the Hollywood Club for a couple of months, the establishment reopened as the Club Kentucky, which most people called the Kentucky Club. The Washingtonians gradually expanded and for a few months featured the great soprano-saxophonist Sidney Bechet (one of the first important jazz soloists), although he never did record with Ellington.

In the spring of 1925, Ellington and Jo Trent learned that the all-black revue *Chocolate Kiddies* needed songs, so they wrote an entire score in one evening. Sam Wooding's Orchestra toured Europe successfully for two years with *Chocolate Kiddies*, although none of the tunes ultimately caught on.

Duke Ellington's Kentucky Club Orchestra (as it was often called during the era) occasionally played at other clubs and took brief road trips. A tour of New England in the summer of 1926 found the band (which was now ten pieces) solidifying its sound and becoming much stronger. A major new asset was trombonist Joe "Tricky Sam" Nanton, who joined Miley in creating a bewildering array of sounds and tones through his inventive work with plunger mutes. With Miley and Nanton dominating the ensembles, Hardwick adding a bit of sweetness, Bass Edwards' tuba helping out the rhythm section, and Louis Metcalf filling in well as second trumpeter (and occasional soloist), the Ellington orchestra was far ahead of its records to date and was quickly becoming a major force to be reckoned with.

Producer Irving Mills, who had met Duke Ellington three years earlier, was very impressed by the improvement in the band, and he helped set up their first recording date with a major record label, Brunswick. On November 29, 1926, the group made their first great recordings: the haunting "East St. Louis Toodle-oo"—Duke's

The master of the plunger mute, Tricky Sam Nanton was unparalleled at expressing emotions and developing unusual sounds on the trombone. He and Bubber Miley originated the "jungle" sound, and Nanton lasted long enough to be a part of the Ray Nance era in the 1940s.

original theme song—and the cooking "Birmingham Breakdown." Irving Mills soon became Duke's manager.

The year 1927 was the band's breakthrough year. Mills secured a lengthy series of recordings, and most are quite memorable. In addition to remaking "East St. Louis Toodle-oo" three times (each version has a slightly different arrangement), Duke debuted "Black and Tan Fantasy," a fascinating work that includes a classic quote from Chopin's "Death March," and "Creole Love Call," which utilizes Adelaide Hall's voice as a wordless instrument. Rudy Jackson joined the band as their first regular clarinet soloist, Wellman Braud (one of the strongest bassists of the era) helped Ellington develop one of the top rhythm sections of the late 1920s, and baritonist

Harry Carney, who had a huge tone and a dexterity on his instrument that was comparable to a tenor, was the first important jazz soloist on the baritone sax. The most loyal of Ellington's sidemen (in later years Duke would be a constant passenger in his car), Carney was with the Ellington orchestra for forty-seven years, staying even after the leader's death.

OPPOSITE: A decent if not virtuosic timekeeper, drummer Sonny Greer added colorful percussive sounds to Duke Ellington's orchestra for twenty-five years and was one of his first musical associates. ABOVE: The Duke Ellington orchestra in 1930 and 1931 was quite an all-star outfit. On trombones are (left to right) Tricky Sam Nanton and Juan Tizol; the trumpeters include Freddy Jenkins, Cootie Williams, and Arthur Whetsol; the reeds are Harry Carney, Johnny Hodges, and Barney Bigard; and, in addition to Ellington, the rhythm section consists of drummer Sonny Greer, Freddy Guy (seen here on banjo), and bassist Wellman Braud.

Harry Carney (the first major soloist on his instrument) joined the band in the autumn. Carney would remain with Duke's orchestra for forty-seven years, even after the leader's passing, until his own death in October 1974.

After nearly four years at the Kentucky Club, Duke Ellington and his orchestra ended their association with the club, again toured the northeast, and played some New York theaters. On December 4, 1927, the orchestra was scheduled to audition along with several other groups at the Cotton Club. Ellington, who was always lax about disciplining his sidemen, showed up late, his men even later; fortunately, the Cotton Club's boss was the latest of all. Since all of the other bands had already departed in disgust, Duke and his orchestra were given a chance to show off their talents and they were hired.

This was Ellington's biggest break. During the next few years, his orchestra would become well known broadcasting from the Cotton Club; in fact, they were soon billed on some records as Duke Ellington and his Famous Orchestra. Because new material was constantly needed for the shows (even with the full-time composing of Jimmy McHugh and lyricist Dorothy Fields), Ellington's writing was in great demand and his talents developed quickly. And, thanks to Mills' connections, the big band recorded constantly, often making multiple versions—for different labels and under different names (one of which was the Jungle Band)—of Duke's compositions, which helped the classic songs to catch on. Sales of sheet music also helped to popularize Ellington's work, in addition to earning him substantial royalties.

In 1931, the Duke Ellington Orchestra, celebrating their fourth year at the Cotton Club, had no real competition. All eight of the horn players in this picture had distinctive sounds, and the rhythm section—drummer Sonny Greer, Ellington, guitarist Fred Guy, and bassist Wellman Braud—was arguably the best in the business.

Altoist Johnny Hodges, who would soon be the pacesetter on his instrument, joined Ellington in 1928 for what would be (with just a three-year interruption in the 1950s) a forty-two-year run. Clarinetist Barney Bigard replaced Rudy Jackson and stayed fourteen years, and Whetsol (taking Louis Metcalf's place) returned. While most jazz bands of the time had two or three main soloists, by late 1928 Duke's orchestra had seven. That year saw the introduction of such notable Ellington pieces as "Black Beauty" (one of the first songs to celebrate African-Americans in its title), "Jubilee Stomp," "Diga Diga Doo," "I Must Have That Man," and most notably, "The Mooche."

The Duke Ellington story would not make a very dramatic movie for, after his initial breakthrough at the Cotton Club, there was no real decline in either Duke's artistic abilities or his popularity (other than a brief period in the early 1950s)—success followed success. There was a slight setback, though. Bubber Miley, Ellington's top soloist and the inspiration for the entire Jungle Band sound, had become increasingly unreliable due to alcoholism. In January 1929, after he had missed one performance too many, Duke reluctantly was forced to fire the influential trumpeter. Miley's remaining three years were a downward spiral that ended with his premature death.

His replacement was Cootie Williams, a superior trumpeter who had formerly worked with Fletcher Henderson's orchestra. After a few gigs in which he played open horn, Williams realized that it was up to him to assume Miley's role and soon he, too, became a master with the mutes, even surpassing his predecessor. Cootie would be one of the main stars with Ellington during two

The legendary Cotton Club, whose elaborate floor shows were performed exclusively by black musicians, singers, and dancers for an all-white audience, was home base for Ellington from 1927 until 1932. It was a superb training ground for his composing talents.

long periods, joining Whetsol (whose quiet and thoughtful style was a perfect contrast), Nanton, Hodges, Bigard, Carney, Guy, Braud, Greer, Ellington himself, and two new additions: Freddy Jenkins, whose Louis Armstrong–inspired solos were an asset, became the band's third trumpeter, and Juan Tizol, who played valve trombone. Though Tizol was not a major soloist, he was a technically skilled musician who could play anyone's part (sometimes filling in for a missing reed player) and was an occasional composer, who later wrote "Caravan" and "Perdido."

Among the notable compositions that were debuted on Duke's recordings during the post-Miley era from 1929 to 1931 were "Cotton Club Stomp," "Wall Street Wail" (recorded shortly after the stock-market crash), "Double Check Stomp," "Old Man Blues," "Rockin' in Rhythm," and the timeless "Mood Indigo," which was arguably Ellington's greatest hit.

Cootie Williams replaced Bubber Miley as Ellington's trumpet plunger specialist in early 1929. A star with Duke for eleven years, Cootie "retired" for twenty-two years and then returned to replace Ray Nance (who had been his successor) for a dozen additional years.

As Ellington's fame spread, he was given his first opportunity to appear on film. Unlike other African-American artists of the 1920s, '30s, and '40s, Duke Ellington was never cast in the role of a buffoon or a servant who provided comic relief. He always had a distinguished air about him and, unlike other talented performers who simply played instruments, sang, or tap-danced, it seemed obvious even to much of the white population in the late 1920s that Duke was probably a genius and certainly deserved respect. Ellington was not completely immune from racism, but at least it never affected his appearances in movies. Duke debuted in the 1929 short *Black and Tan*, in which he leads his big band, plays a duet with Arthur Whetsol, and speaks a few lines; dancer Fredi Washington (who is depicted passing away during the final version of the funeral section of "Black and Tan Fantasy") is the star of the eighteen-minute film.

In 1930, the Duke Ellington orchestra appeared in the full-length Amos 'n' Andy movie *Check and Double Check*, making them the first black big band with a credited appearance in a white feature film. Although the movie itself is a disappointment and quite dated, Ellington's orchestra is seen in a full-length version of "Old Man Blues," with prominent solos from Carney, Hodges, and Jenkins.

The early years of the Depression were a very bleak time for many of the top black jazz musicians, such as King Oliver and Jelly Roll Morton. However, due to his secure engagement at the Cotton Club, the brilliance of his orchestra, and his increasing popularity, Duke Ellington did not have a shortage of work and he was well equipped to "battle" the many new bands (and potential competitors) that would emerge a few years later during the swing era.

ABOVE: Barney Bigard added a New Orleans clarinet sound to Ellington's ensembles during his fifteen years with Duke. His later years, although they included a long stint with Louis Armstrong, were anticlimactic, for only Ellington knew how to showcase Bigard's strengths properly.
OPPOSITE: Johnny Hodges, the top altoist of the swing era and one of the greatest of all time, was Ellington's most popular soloist. As skilled as he was on up-tempo tunes and blues, Hodges was most renowned for his luscious tone and his beautiful renditions of ballads.

Duke Ellington's first appearance on film was in the African-American short *Black and Tan*, which featured Fredi Washington, Ellington, and Arthur Whetsol, along with plenty of dancing girls, who performed Cotton Club–style numbers.

LEFT: In Culver City, California, to participate in the filming of the full-length Amos 'n' Andy film *Check and Double Check*, Duke Ellington humorously stands on a chair to conduct his orchestra; Sonny Greer is seen just playing brushes on a snare drum. One wonders where the piano was.... **ABOVE:** A publicity photo from Ellington's 1930 visit to Hollywood shows the suave bandleader playing up his appeal to women. Followers of Ellington know that he would never have run away from a group of ladies—he would have tried to charm each one individually.

THE SWING ERA

CHAPTER 3

A popular attraction at theaters and already a living legend by the start of the swing era, Duke Ellington is seen here onstage in England at the London Palladium in 1933. His British concerts received mixed reviews until he decided to play his most sophisticated material.

Many consider that the swing era began when Benny Goodman scored an unexpected success at Los Angeles' Palomar Ballroom in 1935, causing dancing teenagers to almost start a riot in response to his swinging music. Although that event did cause the number of big bands to multiply during the next few years as swing began to dominate popular music, there were earlier swinging big bands: Fletcher Henderson's, for instance, which began to swing when Louis Armstrong joined in 1924, and Duke Ellington's, which had been swinging since 1927. In fact, in 1932 Ellington recorded a song that seemed to predict what was going to occur: "It Don't Mean a Thing (If It Ain't Got That Swing)."

The Fletcher Henderson orchestra helped introduce swing to New York. Thanks in large part to their main cornetist Louis Armstrong (back row, third from the left), they were the first major jazz big band. Other notables in this 1924 photo include trombonist Charlie Green (back row, far left), tenor-saxophonist Coleman Hawkins (front row, second from the left), and the innovative arranger Don Redman (front row, fourth from the left); the leader is seated at the piano.

With the onset of the Depression, two forms of inexpensive entertainment rose to prominence: the radio and dance bands. In the early 1930s, the majority of the big bands specialized in commercial ballads and novelties for audiences at dance halls, but some jazz-oriented orchestras (particularly those with a strong home base) were also active, most notably Henderson's, the Casa Loma Orchestra, Cab Calloway's, and Ellington's.

ABOVE, LEFT: Ivie Anderson was Duke Ellington's most respected singer. Starting off in 1932 with "It Don't Mean a Thing (If It Ain't Got That Swing)," which was her first recording, Anderson performed ballads, including "Stormy Weather," novelties, and stomps with equal talent and enthusiasm during her decade with Duke. **ABOVE:** Duke Ellington, who always looked sophisticated, really outdid himself in 1934, sporting a high hat and a typically up-to-date outfit. No wonder he successfully countered all stereotypes!

By 1932, Calloway's orchestra had replaced Duke Ellington's as the house band at the Cotton Club, although Ellington, for the remainder of the decade, would occasionally return "home." From this point on his orchestra was largely a road band and, despite some long residencies, would remain so for more than four decades.

The recording of "It Don't Mean a Thing" was important in three ways: it predicted the swing era, it became a timeless hit, and it was the debut recording for Ivie Anderson, who would be Duke's official vocalist until 1942. A sophisticated

In the summer of 1933, Ellington and his orchestra began their first European tour with two weeks of shows at the Palladium in London. On the day of the band's first appearance, the theater broke all prior box-office records.

singer with a subtle style, Anderson was able to interpret ballads and more up-tempo tunes with equal skill and is today often thought of as Ellington's finest singer, although she remains quite underrated in the rest of the music world, especially considering that she had a serious solo career as well.

The 1932–1934 period (which preceded the beginning of the swing era) was typically productive for Ellington. Among the many notable recordings were inventive reworkings of "Bugle Call Rag," "Rose Room," and "The Sheik of Araby" (which became a notable feature for trombonist Lawrence Brown, the newest addition to Ellington's orchestra), along with such new songs as "Sophisticated Lady," "Drop Me Off in Harlem," "Stompy Jones," "Solitude," and the remarkable "Daybreak Express." The latter was the greatest of all Ellington's train songs, for his innovative arrangement had his orchestra musically depict a train ride from beginning to end, complete with train whistles, the sound of wheels churning, and the pure excitement of travel.

In 1933, Duke and his band appeared in Europe for the first time, touring England, France, and the Netherlands. The first part of their visit to Great Britain was only a mixed success because Ellington featured a Cotton Club–type entertainment show. To his surprise, the British public was more interested in his "serious" music. Unaccustomed to being treated as a great artist rather than as a mere entertainer, Ellington eventually adjusted his band's performance and the reviews improved greatly.

That same year the Duke Ellington orchestra was featured in a nine-minute film short, *A Bundle of Blues*, highlighted by a lengthy rendition of "Stormy Weather" that starred Ivie Anderson. In 1934, they had small parts in three other films: *Murder at the Vanities*, offscreen in the Burns and Allen movie *Many Happy Returns*, and more prominently in the Mae West feature *Belle of the Nineties*, where they helped the actress introduce "My Old Flame." The most impressive of their film appearances from this period was *Symphony in Black: A Rhapsody of Negro Life*, which in nine minutes depicts four aspects of 1930s African-American life: "The Laborers" (the difficulty of manual labor), "A Triangle" (a brief love story), "A Hymn of Sorrow" (a congregation mourning the death of a baby), and "Harlem Rhythm" (the joys of Saturday night). In addition to showing off some of Duke's top soloists, this film marked the first appearance of then-unknown singer Billie Holiday in the blues section "A Triangle."

In 1935, Ellington's orchestra featured a new cornetist, Rex Stewart. Otherwise, the personnel was largely unchanged from a few years earlier; from left to right the players are: Wellman Braud, Otto Hardwick, Lawrence Brown, Tricky Sam Nanton, Stewart, Arthur Whetsol, Sonny Greer, Harry Carney, Barney Bigard, Johnny Hodges, Juan Tizol, and Fred Guy. The leader, standing in front, looks rightfully proud.

Before the swing era even officially began, Duke Ellington, thanks in large part to his song hits (several of which had already become standards), was well on his way to becoming a household name. Since he had already established his identity, Ellington, who may not have gotten the biggest headlines during the 1935–1938 period, was able to flourish despite competition from Benny Goodman, Tommy Dorsey, Artie Shaw, Count Basie, and (by 1939) Glenn Miller.

OPPOSITE: Duke Ellington went out of his way to smile anytime he saw a camera around. At the time that this publicity photo was taken in the early 1940s, his orchestra was at the peak of its powers. The other big bands—competitors at the time—would come and go, but Ellington's was one of the few to last for decades. **ABOVE, LEFT:** Ellington and Billie Holiday collaborated only infrequently through the years, including at the 1945 *Esquire* All-Stars concert that resulted in this picture. Lady Day debuted on screen in 1935 in Ellington's short film *Symphony in Black*, singing a memorable blues chorus. **ABOVE:** Ivie Anderson, seen here performing with Duke Ellington's orchestra in 1933, was the first singer to become a regular part of Duke's ensemble. Her classy approach to even low-down blues, along with her general versatility and charming nature, made her a popular attraction.

Among the new songs debuted by Duke during this time period were "In a Sentimental Mood," "Clarinet Lament" (a feature for Barney Bigard), "Echoes of Harlem," "Caravan," "Harmony in Harlem" (which features some wonderful soprano

LEFT: Ellington's Orchestra had nearly the same personnel in 1938 as it had had three years earlier, but Wallace Jones was in Whetsol's spot and Billy Taylor was on bass. Although historians often think of Ellington's 1939–1942 band as being his greatest, this particular outfit was comparable. ABOVE: Duke Ellington, mugging for the camera with someone's flute and string bass in 1934, shows off both his physical strength and his sense of absurdity. It was not until 1969, when Harold Ashby joined, that Ellington utilized the flute in his orchestra.

THE SWING ERA 51

sax from Johnny Hodges), "I Let a Song Go Out of My Heart" (which became one of his best-selling records ever), "Pyramid," and "Prelude to a Kiss." "Boy Meets Horn" showcased the Ellington orchestra's newest soloist, cornetist Rex Stewart, whose ability to play eerie tones by pushing selective valves down only halfway on his horn was utilized by Duke as a fresh voice. Stewart and first trumpeter Wallace Jones (who rarely soloed) replaced the departing Arthur Whetsol and Freddy Jenkins; the

ABOVE: In 1937, when this shot was taken, Duke Ellington had been a major name for a decade. Although he would have been remembered as a legendary composer even if he had called it quits at the time, Ellington had several decades of tremendous musical accomplishments ahead of him. **ABOVE, RIGHT:** Rex Stewart (seen here in 1944) was a real spark plug for Ellington, adding a strong dose of humor with his emotional half-valve notes and competitive spirit. His small-group Ellington combo dates were among the most exciting in the idiom, and his sound stood apart from that of Cootie Williams.

only other personnel change during the four-year period was in the bass spot. Wellman Braud had left early in 1935 and Ellington then experimented with having two bassists: Billy Taylor (no relation to the later pianist) and Hayes Alvis. This was the first time a big band had used two bassists, although in time Taylor was the only one retained.

By 1936, in addition to his steady string of recordings, Ellington was wise enough to sponsor small-group records featuring band members and led by Johnny Hodges, Barney Bigard, Cootie Williams, and Rex Stewart. These combo dates gave the horn players more freedom and publicity (which kept them happy) and allowed Duke, who was usually the pianist, to try out new compositions.

By 1939, Duke Ellington, at age forty, could already look back on a lifetime's worth of achievements, and yet his most productive era was just about to begin.

This rather disorganized photo (could one imagine the Duke Ellington orchestra really performing this way?) is a publicity shot for the obscure film *The Hit Parade*, which starred Frances Langford and featured Ivie Anderson and Ellington's orchestra performing "It Don't Mean a Thing (If It Ain't Got That Swing)."

ABOVE: Cootie Williams, in addition to displaying wizardry with mutes (following and extending the tradition of Bubber Miley), was a superior swing soloist and a master of distinctive sounds with his horn open. When he left Ellington in 1940 to join Benny Goodman, the switch was considered major news. **RIGHT:** In a jam session from the late 1930s, rhythm guitarist Fred Guy assists four exceptional musicians: cornetist Rex Stewart (who became famous for his valve technique on "Boy Meets Horn"), Barney Bigard, Cootie Williams, and Tricky Sam Nanton.

THE REMARKABLE BLANTON/WEBSTER/STRAHORN BAND

CHAPTER 4

In the 1942 movie *Reveille with Beverly* (starring Ann Miller), Duke Ellington and his orchestra, pictured with their new singer Betty Roché, performed "Take the 'A' Train" with brio and tongue-in-cheek showmanship.

ineteen thirty-nine was a huge year for Duke Ellington, leading to what many consider to be his greatest period. It was the year that he permanently broke with Irving Mills. Mills had been a tremendous help in getting Ellington's name established, but his habit of listing himself as one of the composers of Duke's songs (an all-too-prevalent practice of agents and some bandleaders) was offensive, and he often urged Ellington to stand still creatively and continue producing "jungle music." Although Duke would always retain some of his early roots in his music, he had a ceaseless desire to move forward and evolve, so Mills' advice was deemed useless. A short European tour that year was Irving Mills' last activity for Ellington.

Three important contributors joined the Duke Ellington orchestra in 1939. The phenomenal young bassist Jimmie Blanton (only twenty at the time) succeeded Billy Taylor. While most other string bassists of the era merely played on the beat, Blanton provided countermelodies and consistently stimulating rhythmic ideas. He was also a major soloist and sounded ten years ahead of his time. Tragically, he died just three years later from tuberculosis, but during his period with Duke, Blanton revolutionized the bass by expanding its role as both accompanist and soloist, which inspired countless young bassists.

Up until 1939, Ellington had never had a major tenor saxophone soloist. Ben Webster was an important addition, for he had a dual musical personality: rough and brutal on up-tempo tunes, yet purring like a kitten on ballads. Although he was

ABOVE: Ben Webster, pictured in 1964 next to the Unisphere that was built for that year's World's Fair in New York, had been a significant addition to Ellington's orchestra twenty-five years earlier. Able to play both heated stomps and romantic ballads, Webster, whose sound was always instantly recognizable, was Ellington's first major tenor saxophone soloist. **OPPOSITE:** The innovative Jimmie Blanton, seen here in 1940, is considered the first "modern" bassist. Rather than assuming a purely supportive role and playing his solos four-to-the-bar as his predecessors had, Blanton performed solos that were as fluent as a guitarist's, and his lines were quite advanced, even in ensembles. Tragically, tuberculosis struck him down in 1942, at the tender age of twenty-four.

Despite the absence of bassist Jimmie Blanton, who was replaced by Junior Raglin, the lineup in 1942 may have been Duke's finest orchestra ever. Pictured from left to right are Harry Carney, Raglin, Otto Hardwick, Fred Guy, Johnny Hodges, Barney Bigard, Ben Webster, Sonny Greer, Juan Tizol, Tricky Sam Nanton, Wallace Jones, Lawrence Brown, and Rex Stewart.

only with Duke for four years, Webster (who ranked with Coleman Hawkins and Lester Young as one of the big three tenor saxists during the period) would always be associated with Ellington.

The third addition to the Ellington fold would be the most important. When performing in Pittsburgh the previous year, Duke had met Billy Strayhorn. Just twenty-three at the time, Strayhorn played Duke a song he had recently composed, called "Lush Life," and Ellington was so impressed that he told Strayhorn to meet him in New York. During the train trip into New York, Strayhorn wrote "Take the 'A' Train," which would soon become Ellington's new theme song, replacing "East St. Louis Toodle-oo." In the course of the next twenty-eight years (until his death in 1967), Billy Strayhorn not only wrote songs for Ellington but became his constant collaborator, and Strayhorn's presence inspired Duke to compose some of his finest work. Through the years, Ellington and Strayhorn collaborated on so many different pieces that it was often difficult to know where one's work finished and the other's began. Although his compositions were sometimes mistakenly attributed to Duke and his own solo career was largely nonexistent due to his dedication to Ellington, Billy Strayhorn has posthumously been recognized as a major composer in his own right.

When one considers that Ellington's orchestra in 1939 also had major soloists in Rex Stewart, Cootie Williams, Tricky Sam Nanton, Lawrence Brown, Barney Bigard, Johnny Hodges, Harry Carney, and Ellington himself, it is not surprising that a great deal of historic music was about to be created. That year saw the birth of such songs as "Portrait of the Lion" (Ellington's tribute to Willie "The Lion" Smith), the catchy "I'm Checkin' Out, Go'om Bye," and Strayhorn's "Something

Sometimes it seemed as if Sonny Greer was as significant for his huge drum/percussion setup as for his actual playing. In this 1940 picture taken at Chicago's Hotel Sherman, Greer's equipment includes gongs, bells, a woodblock, timpani, and vibes.

Barney Bigard and Johnny Hodges pass the time on a train in 1940 playing cards. Despite some lengthy residencies, the orchestra's home was essentially the road after it left the Cotton Club in 1932. Ellington generally only stopped by his New York City apartment to check his mail.

to Live For." The next year found Ellington debuting "Cotton Tail" (which is highlighted by a classic Ben Webster solo), "Concerto for Cootie," "All Too Soon," "Harlem Airshaft," "In a Mellotone," "Warm Valley," "Pitter Panther Patter" (one of several piano-bass duets that were showcases for Blanton), "Flamingo"—a big hit for the band's new male vocalist Herb Jeffries—and three numbers that featured prominent spots for the bassist: "Ko-Ko," "Jack the Bear," and "Sepia Panorama."

There was one possible setback for Duke Ellington in 1940. Cootie Williams, a prime soloist for eleven years, left Ellington to accept an offer with Benny Goodman; within a year he would become a bandleader himself. His defection literally made headlines (in those days swing soloists were considered celebrities), but fortunately Ellington was quickly able to gain the services of Ray Nance, who was not only a fine plunger specialist on the trumpet (like Cootie and Bubber Miley), but a strong violin soloist (the only one Duke ever had) and an excellent singer. Nance went on to be a popular attraction with the band for more than twenty years.

In addition to constant performances and touring during this period, there was a special project that took place during the latter part of 1941. Ellington was involved in a futuristic civil rights play called *Jump for Joy* that ran for twelve weeks in Los Angeles. The cast included actress Dorothy Dandridge, blues singer Big Joe Turner, Duke's singers Ivie Anderson and Herb Jeffries, plus other singers, dancers, comedians, and specialty acts. The show had twelve writers (including Mickey Rooney) and it evolved through each performance. *Jump for Joy* soon passed into history (aside from a brief revival when it was updated in 1959), but several of its songs became standards, including the title cut, "Rocks in My Bed," "Subtle Slough" (later retitled "Squeeze Me but Please Don't Tease Me"), and its main hit, "I Got It Bad and That Ain't Good."

Although overshadowed in popularity polls by Glenn Miller's band and other competitors, the Duke Ellington orchestra remained at the peak of its powers during 1941 and 1942. Among its new recordings were "Take the 'A' Train,"

Duke Ellington and the brilliant Gypsy swing guitarist Django Reinhardt admired each other's talents. Here, Duke and Reinhardt enjoy a jam session at the Hot Club of France in Paris in 1939, along with cornetist Rex Stewart, bassist Louis Vola, and Max Geldray on harmonica.

"I Got It Bad," Strayhorn's beautiful "Chelsea Bridge," "Perdido," "The 'C' Jam Blues," and "What Am I Here For." A recording strike by the Musicians Union kept Ellington's orchestra from recording from July 1942 until his label, RCA Victor, settled in November 1944, but his big band stayed busy. They toured constantly and appeared in the all-black musical film *Cabin in the Sky* (which starred Ethel Waters and Lena Horne) in addition to playing "Take the 'A' Train" in the Ann Miller movie *Reveille with Beverly*.

Ellington's futuristic civil rights play *Jump for Joy* had only a short run in Los Angeles in 1941 before it slipped away into history. Here, Jimmie Blanton, Duke, and singer Herb Jeffries perform in the orchestra pit during the legendary play.

At Last on the Screen! The Musical Comedy Sensation!

CABIN IN THE SKY

Starring
★ ETHEL WATERS ★ Eddie "ROCHESTER" Anderson
(famed Torch Singer) (Funnier Than Ever)
★ LENA HORNE
(Gorgeous Song-Bird)
with LOUIS ARMSTRONG ★ REX INGRAM ★ DUKE ELLINGTON AND HIS ORCHESTRA
★ THE HALL JOHNSON CHOIR

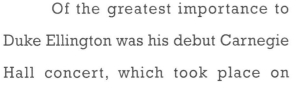

A Metro-Goldwyn-Mayer PICTURE
SCA®

ABOVE, LEFT: The 1942 movie *Cabin in the Sky* had a stellar all-black cast, although the story included some typical racial stereotypes. Ellington's orchestra was featured in two numbers: "Goin' Up" and "Things Ain't What They Used to Be." **ABOVE:** Ellington loved to check out other musicians' performances during his off hours. At Café Society in 1943, Duke and pianist Teddy Wilson, who had a long residency at the club, are joined by Orson Welles and Cab Calloway. Welles reportedly said that Ellington was the only genius he knew—other than himself.

Of the greatest importance to Duke Ellington was his debut Carnegie Hall concert, which took place on January 23, 1943. Ellington had long been interested in writing extended compositions that were weightier than the three-minute masterpieces featured on his records. The 78 rpm record forced performers to be very concise in the pre-LP era, but Ellington found ways to get around its limitations: as early as 1929, he had recorded a two-sided six-minute version of "Tiger Rag." While that was primarily a jam session, 1931's "Creole Rhapsody" was a six-minute composition; the four-part "Reminiscing in Tempo" (written in memory of his mother after her death in 1935) went on for twelve. But these were merely brief preludes to "Black, Brown, and Beige."

Subtitled "A Tone Parallel to the History of the American Negro," the forty-seven-minute "Black, Brown, and Beige" premiered at the Carnegie Hall concert to the delight of some listeners and the mystification of others. Critics at the time complained that it was neither classical music nor all-out jazz. Ellington concurred, saying that he did not want to fit easily into any category. Some sections of the suite became well-known independently of the work, most notably a spiritual

During her six years with Ellington, Kay Davis expanded upon the role that Adelaide Hall had founded with "Creole Love Call" in 1928—that of a wordless vocalist whose voice would be utilized as part of the ensembles and for effects. Her best-known recordings were "Transbluency" and "On a Turquoise Cloud." Davis retired from singing in 1950.

melody played beautifully by Johnny Hodges that became known as "Come Sunday," and "The Blues," which had some memorable vocalizing by Betty Roché. Due to the strong criticism, which stung, Ellington later performed only excerpts of "Black, Brown, and Beige," but the piece in its original format is a gem. He never made a commercial recording of the entire work, although a live recording of the Carnegie Hall concert was finally released in 1977.

In addition to his group's regular repertoire, Ellington's series of Carnegie Hall concerts (which were usually annual events through 1948) gave him an opportunity to debut new extensive works, including the four-part "Perfume Suite" (1944), "A Tonal Group" (1946), "The Deep South Suite (1946), "The Liberian Suite" (1947), and "The Tattooed Bride" (1948). These concerts helped to remind fans that Duke Ellington was no ordinary band-leader or musician.

Dr. Billy Taylor, the famous pianist and spokesman for jazz, remembers meeting Duke Ellington in the mid-1940s.

"When I first came to New York, I played with Ben Webster, who introduced me to Duke. He was very kind to me, as he always was to younger players, encouraging me in a lot of ways. I tried not to ask him too much about music, but I remember one time I was curious about a strange modulation that he made, and asked him how he had thought of going from one chord to another chord in such an odd way. He told me that the key for him was the day that he realized that C-sharp was different than D-flat! That was when he realized that he could write anything."

The World War II years proved quite difficult for many of the big bands. Travel restrictions and gasoline shortages made it harder for orchestras to make appearances, and the draft caused a lot of turnover. Duke Ellington's orchestra was hurt a bit in those areas but most of its departures would have occurred anyway. Blanton's death resulted in the bass spot being filled first by Junior Raglin and then by the great Oscar Pettiford, a bebop innovator who was Blanton's natural successor. When clarinetist Barney Bigard tired of the road in 1942, it took nearly a year to find a permanent replacement, but Jimmy Hamilton then remained for the next twenty-five years. Ivie Anderson also departed in 1942 due to ill health. She was replaced by several singers in the short run, including Joya Sherrill, the operatic Kay Davis, and Betty Roché, but no one could quite take her place.

Jimmy Hamilton, seen here in 1944, had a cool, almost cold tone and a fluent style that was influenced by bop. Because he sounded very different from his predecessor, Barney Bigard, there was some opposition among longtime Ellington fans, but Russell Procope, who could sound like a New Orleans clarinetist, eventually filled the void, while Hamilton blazed new paths on pieces such as "Air Conditioned Jungle."

Despite the problems caused by World War II and the competition from countless other big bands, Duke Ellington's orchestra occupied its own niche and was considered by most informed listeners to be a cut above the other ensembles. The leader's songs (and increasingly the originals of Billy Strayhorn) were often played by other groups (Harry James had a major hit with Duke's "I'm Beginning to See the Light"), his arranging techniques were influential—if rarely successfully duplicated—and his sidemen constantly voted "most popular" in readers' polls. Although the musical landscape would soon change drastically, Duke Ellington still had three decades of significant musical accomplishments ahead of him.

SWIMMING
AGAINST THE TIDE

CHAPTER 5

Ellington's orchestra had to struggle to stay afloat in the late 1940s, when business for big bands began to decline in the United States. In 1950, Duke took the orchestra on a tour of Europe, where he still received huge welcomes, such as this one at the Milan railway station.

By early 1945, the lineup of the Duke Ellington Orchestra had changed a bit but was still mostly intact. In addition to Ray Nance and Rex Stewart, the trumpet section included the advanced swing soloist Taft Jordan and the remarkable high-note trumpeter—possibly the finest ever—Cat Anderson, who added a tremendous amount to the ensembles. Juan Tizol had left, but Tricky Sam Nanton and Lawrence Brown were still in the trombone section and the saxophones included Johnny Hodges, Harry Carney, Jimmy Hamilton, Otto Hardwick, and Al Sears, a fine rhythm and blues–oriented tenor player who replaced Ben Webster. Duke was joined by former Washingtonians Fred Guy and Sonny Greer in the rhythm section, and bassist Junior Raglin.

Ray Nance, who replaced Cootie Williams when he departed after an eleven-year run, was a triple threat. Not only was he a fine cornetist, making his mark with a famous solo on the original recording of "Take the 'A' Train," but he was a talented jazz violinist and a very likable singer. He would be one of Ellington's major attractions throughout the 1940s and '50s.

The band had new hits in "Don't Get Around Much Anymore," "Things Ain't What They Used to Be" (the best-known composition by Duke's son, Mercer Ellington), "I Ain't Got Nothing but the Blues" (a feature for Duke's new singer Al Hibbler), and "I Didn't Know About You." Don George, who worked with Ellington frequently during this era, proved to be one of Duke's finest lyricists. But, to the surprise of nearly everyone, the swing era was about to end and the music world was on the verge of great changes.

After ten years of dominating popular music, the big band must have seemed like a permanent fixture, but the situation soon changed. Most big bands broke up as the result of many factors. The recording strike of 1942–1944 kept jazz musicians off records for a long period. This left the door open to singers such as Frank Sinatra, Perry Como, and Doris Day, who were not included in the

Even during the harder times, when his orchestra was fighting against the odds, Duke Ellington found much to be happy about. The music was always happening, the royalty checks from his earlier hit songs gave him an advantage over other swing-era bandleaders, and there was the joy of constant creativity.

strike and soon became major attractions as a result. A ruinous entertainment tax made it very expensive for ballrooms to hire large orchestras and, in the postwar era, musicians became weary of traveling endlessly for low pay. The dancing audience shifted from the big bands to either the ballad-oriented singers or smaller rhythm and blues combos. The jazz audience became divided between the revival of Dixieland and the newer bebop, which greatly interested younger musicians and arrangers. And, after a decade, most big swing bands were simply running out of new ideas.

Cat Anderson was quite possibly the greatest high-note trumpeter that jazz has ever had. His stratospheric notes were generally perfectly in tune and, during his periods with Ellington between 1944 and 1971, his presence allowed Duke to write confidently in the extreme top register of the trumpet, knowing full well that it would cause Cat no problems.

OPPOSITE: Trombonist Lawrence Brown and altoist Johnny Hodges were two of the three defectors—drummer Sonny Greer was the third—whose departure in 1951 made some observers wonder whether Duke Ellington's best days were behind him. But that was before the "Great James Robbery," when Duke wooed three musicians away from Harry James' band.
ABOVE: *Symphony in Swing*, an obscure but historic short film, gave the 1949 Duke Ellington orchestra, one of his lesser-known groups, an opportunity to show off some of their assets. Along with the leader on his elevated piano are (from the left) trombonists Quentin Jackson and Tyree Glenn, singer Kay Davis, altoist Johnny Hodges, clarinetist Jimmy Hamilton, and tenor great Ben Webster, who was temporarily back with Ellington.

By the end of the 1940s, very few big bands were operating on a full-time basis. Even such luminaries as Benny Goodman, Artie Shaw, Gene Krupa, and Cab Calloway no longer had regular orchestras. Glenn Miller and Jimmy Lunceford had died, Tommy and Jimmy Dorsey had to combine their two bands into one, and in early 1950, Count Basie was forced to temporarily cut back to a combo. The more noteworthy big bands of the era, those led by Woody Herman,

Stan Kenton, and Dizzy Gillespie, were generally together for only a couple years before breaking up or reforming, and the few remaining veteran orchestras were often reduced to playing nostalgic favorites.

Despite the high musical quality of his ensemble and the song royalties brought in by his many hits that enabled Ellington to keep his orchestra together, the decade from 1945 to 1955 was a difficult one for Duke Ellington, too. Even though he remained a household name, Duke was overshadowed by the bebop innovators, the pop singers, and eventually the teenage rock and roll stars. Somehow, he survived.

In 1946, Ellington faced another disappointment with the failure of *Beggar's Holiday*, a Broadway show that he, Billy Strayhorn, and lyricist John LaTouce collaborated on. This photo from the same year shows Duke the composer hard at work.

LEFT: Although Duke was hardly thought of as a rock musician, he somehow managed to get the orchestra included in this revue, along with such popular performers as Nat King Cole. **ABOVE:** During the upheaval of the first half of the 1950s, these were four of Ellington's most loyal sidemen: Harry Carney, Billy Strayhorn, tenor saxophonist Paul Gonsalves, and Ray Nance. All could have had lucrative years as soloists but chose to stay with Ellington—in the case of the first three, until their deaths—because they knew that they had found their musical home.

The Duke Ellington orchestra was quite strong in 1945 and, despite frequent personnel changes, it would remain so during this period. The following year did result in a couple of major losses. Altoist Otto Hardwick (who was underutilized by Duke due to the presence of the brilliant Johnny Hodges) retired and, on July 21, Tricky Sam Nanton died suddenly. Nanton's expertise with plunger mutes, such a major part of Ellington's sound, has never been duplicated but his spot in later years would be filled by other trombonists who could come close, most notably Tyree Glenn (who doubled on vibraphone) and, in the 1950s, Quentin Jackson.

In 1946, the great Gypsy guitarist Django Reinhardt made his only American tour, accompanied by Ellington's orchestra. Unfortunately, Django did not adjust well to the discipline of travel and concerts; on a couple of occasions he ran across old friends and did not show up for the performances. Another project that was not overly successful was the play *Beggar's Holiday* (based on the classic *Beggar's Opera*), for which Ellington and Strayhorn reportedly wrote seventy-nine songs. The show appeared on Broadway for a brief run of 108 performances, and most of the music has since been forgotten; Duke only recorded five of the songs, none of which caught on.

Such failures were infrequent, however. Ellington's orchestra continued performing on a nightly basis and, although the audience was starting to shrink, the music remained unique and innovative. The band's style was opening up a bit toward the chordal, rhythmic, and harmonic innovations of bebop but without losing its own distinctive sound. Bop bassist Oscar Pettiford, who was a member of the orchestra during this period, was a factor in this evolution. While occasionally looking backward to his roots in stride piano, Duke's keyboard style was becoming more percussive and was invariably modern. In his composition "The Clothed Woman" from 1947, Duke flirted with atonality, and years later, when he heard a record by Thelonious Monk, he would state half-jokingly that Monk was stealing his stuff.

Among the songs recorded by Ellington during 1946 and 1947 were the very catchy "Tulip or Turnip" (featuring Ray Nance on vocals), "Sultry Serenade," Jimmy Hamilton's feature on the adventurous "Air Conditioned Jungle," and "Happy Go Lucky Local"; the last section of the latter would be "borrowed" by tenor

During the 1940s and '50s, the team of Ellington and Strayhorn gave Duke's orchestra a consistently fresh repertoire, resulting in a hit song ("Satin Doll") and many ambitious suites, plus reworkings of older Ellington standards.

saxophonist Jimmy Forrest (who was with Ellington in 1949) and retitled "Night Train," a huge (if uncredited) hit of the early 1950s. Another major piece was 1947's "Liberian Suite," which, in addition to featuring several of the musicians instrumentally (including Nance on violin and Glenn on vibes), included the warm ballad "I Like the Sunrise." Although identified with the swing era, Duke Ellington always kept his ears open to newer sounds. Sometime in the late 1940s he offered the innovative altoist Charlie "Bird" Parker a position with his band. However, Parker asked for so much money that Ellington commented that if the altoist would pay him that much, he would give up his band and become Bird's pianist!

Ellington was able to keep his name before the public with extensive touring and frequent appearances on radio programs. Many new musicians passed through his band at this time. Bassist Wendell Marshall (a cousin of the late Jimmie Blanton) joined the orchestra and would stay for six years. Harold "Shorty" Baker held down the lyrical trumpet chair founded by Arthur Whetsol. Al Killian was the band's high-note trumpeter (taking over during a Cat Anderson hiatus), and Lawrence Brown was joined in the trombone section by both Tyree Glenn (who would leave by 1950) and Quentin Jackson. The

Duke Ellington's charisma carried over the radio—he didn't need to see an audience to enchant it with his smooth voice and witty remarks. Frequent appearances on radio programs helped the orchestra maintain its status as a household name at a time when the popularity of other big bands was waning.

sax section remained largely intact with Johnny Hodges, Jimmy Hamilton, and Harry Carney. Russell Procope was Otto Hardwick's permanent replacement and, although a fine altoist, his New Orleans–style clarinet work (a major contrast to Hamilton's cooler boppish style) would become his trademark in the band.

When the popular tenorman Al Sears departed in 1949, a couple of younger modernists—Charlie Rouse, who would later play with Thelonious Monk, and Jimmy Forrest—filled in for a time. In 1950, Paul Gonsalves, who would play an important part in Ellington's renaissance a few years later, became the band's permanent tenor soloist.

The Duke Ellington orchestra in 1951 would have to be ranked near the top of all active big bands, but even so there were some problems. Ellington and Strayhorn, while composing many enduring longer works, had not had a hit record in some time and only one (1953's "Satin Doll," which would take several years to catch on) was in the near future. A European tour in 1950 (Ellington's first real tour since 1939) was successful, but a potential disaster occurred in early 1951.

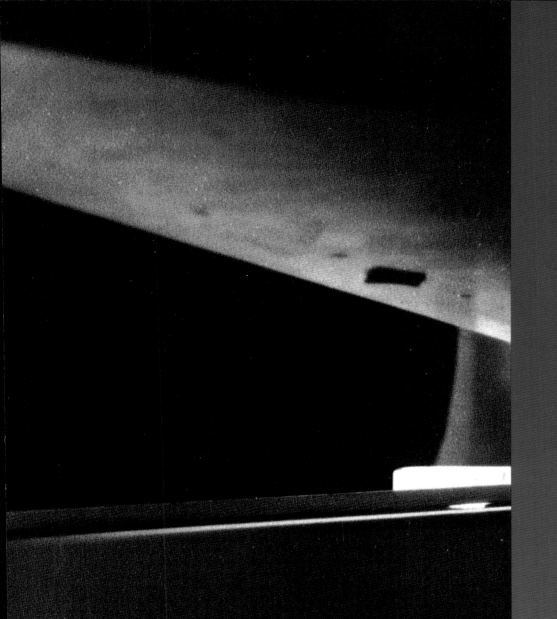

LEFT: In 1953, Duke Ellington recorded his first full-length trio album, *The Duke Plays Ellington* (later retitled *Piano Reflections*). On this date—and nine years later on *Money Jungle*—he showed how modern his piano playing remained, incorporating dissonance and advanced harmonies that indirectly influenced Thelonious Monk and Cecil Taylor. **TOP:** Juan Tizol, a technically skilled valve trombonist, was with Ellington from 1929 until 1944, during which time he composed "Caravan" and "Perdido." Tizol's musical fluency made it possible for him to fill in for any missing saxophonists or trumpeters. **ABOVE:** Throughout the 1950s, Ray Nance remained one of Ellington's most consistent players and, particularly during periods of great turnover, was a stabilizing influence. His swing-style trumpet was a strong contrast to the more boppish flights of Clark Terry and Willie Cook.

Clark Terry, who had played with Count Basie in the late 1940s, was one of the top new voices with Duke Ellington in the 1950s. His fluent trumpet style (falling between swing and bop), exuberant tone, and high musicianship made him one of Ellington's strongest and most reliable soloists of the decade—he was often well featured on "Perdido."

Altoist Johnny Hodges, who had been Duke's top soloist since 1928, decided to form his own combo and he took along trombonist Lawrence Brown (with Ellington since 1931) and drummer Sonny Greer, the last of the original Washingtonians. Hodges, whose beautiful tone was equally rewarding on ballads, blues, and stomps, was a major loss.

It took about two months, but Duke solved his problem with what was called "The Great James Robbery." He convinced valve trombonist Juan Tizol (a former Ellington orchestra member), altoist Willie Smith, and drummer Louie Bellson to leave Harry James' band. Actually this raid was of a friendly nature, since James was only working part-time during the period and the agreement was for the musicians to stay just a year. Tizol was never a major soloist, but his presence helped solidify Ellington's band. Smith, one of the top altoists of the 1930s, was a logical choice to fill Hodges' spot, while Bellson added a new vitality to the orchestra. One of the great drum virtuosos, Bellson was also a fine composer whose writing was an asset to the band during his stay, and his drum solos added to the orchestra's appeal. Other important acquisitions in 1950 included Clark Terry and Willie Cook, who joined Ray Nance and the returning Cat Anderson to give Ellington four talented but very different trumpet soloists.

Despite the difficulties of keeping the band together during an era when jazz orchestras were becoming largely extinct, the period from 1950 to 1952 resulted in some classic music. The rise of the LP allowed Ellington to document some of his lengthier pieces more easily, including "A Tone Parallel to Harlem" (also known as simply "Harlem") and "The Tattooed Bride." One highly praised album, *Ellington Uptown*, includes Louie Bellson's drum feature "Skin Deep," a memorable rendition of "Take the 'A' Train" that is highlighted by a humorous vocal by Betty Roché (who was temporarily back

A transitional version of the Duke Ellington orchestra jams in Paris in 1950. Ellington provides percussion for the group: high-note trumpeter Al Killian, clarinetist Jimmy Hamilton, singer Kay Davis, clarinetist Russell Procope, trombonist Quentin Jackson, tenorman Alva "Bo" McCain, trumpeters Nelson "Cadillac" Williams and Ernie Royal, and Billy Strayhorn.

in the band), "The Controversial Suite" (which looked back at New Orleans jazz and ahead toward a potentially menacing future), and definitive renditions of "Perdido" and "The Mooche."

Although the Duke Ellington orchestra kept busy from 1953 through 1955, this was a low-profile period. The band actually spent the summer of 1955 backing other acts at an Aquacade show in New York. This anonymous gig was considered a low point in Duke's career, although it did allow the band to keep working. Even with ten major soloists (including trombonist Britt Woodman, who had joined in 1951), at this point the chances were only moderate that the Duke Ellington orchestra would last to the end of the decade. But then came the 1956 Newport Jazz Festival.

RENAISSANCE

CHAPTER 6

The pleasure of improvised music and constant creativity was at the heart of Duke Ellington's remarkable career for more than half a century.

hings began to look up for Duke Ellington late in 1955. Johnny Hodges, after four years as the leader of a small combo that had a hit in "Castle Rock," returned to Ellington's orchestra, where he would remain for his last fifteen years. With drummer Sam Woodyard and bassist Jimmy Woode as new members of the rhythm section, the Ellington band had no weak spots. All it needed was for the rest of the world to be reminded of its greatness.

On July 7, 1956, the Duke Ellington orchestra debuted the new "Newport Jazz Festival Suite" at the Newport Jazz Festival and performed a few of its standards. The applause was respectful. To conclude the set, Duke performed a couple of obscure ensemble-oriented pieces from 1937: "Diminuendo in Blue" and "Crescendo in Blue." Connecting them was a "wailing interlude" that found tenor saxophonist Paul Gonsalves playing twenty-seven choruses on a medium-tempo blues. By his tenth chorus the crowd was going wild, dancing madly and nearly starting a riot. The performance made headlines and overnight Duke Ellington was a major name again. Two months later Duke was on the cover of *Time* magazine. The momentum caused by this concert would never falter, and there was no longer any talk of Ellington breaking up his orchestra.

OPPOSITE: The master in an introspective pose. Given the choice of thinking about past glories or looking ahead to new innovations, Duke Ellington would always choose the latter. ABOVE: The perfect showman, Ellington knew how to excite an audience, involving them in the music that he and the orchestra were creating on stage.

Now fifty-seven, Duke Ellington had long since graduated from being a mere big band leader and composer into a living legend. During the next seventeen years, he would have one success after another, and he would not have to compete with anyone but himself. A 1957 television production, the fanciful *A Drum Is a Woman*, got mixed reviews, but a European tour

One of Ellington's few speaking roles in a major motion picture was in 1959's *Anatomy of a Murder*, in which he spoke a few lines in one scene after playing a bit of four-handed piano with the film's star, Jimmy Stewart. More significantly, Ellington wrote the highly rated film score.

the following year was a triumph; Duke would soon be revisiting the continent on a regular basis. The soundtrack Ellington composed for the 1959 Jimmy Stewart film *Anatomy of a Murder* was quite successful, and he made a brief appearance on screen as well. The pattern was now set and would continue throughout the 1960s: constant touring both in the United States and abroad (playing clubs and festivals), many recordings (quite a few of which would not be released until after Ellington's death), television appearances, occasional movie work, and some unusual projects.

There were many major events and collaborations. Ellington made recordings with Louis Armstrong's All-Stars (a successful 1961 encounter, although it is a shame that the trumpeter never had a chance to return the favor and record with Duke's big band); as a trio with Charles Mingus and Max Roach; with the immortal tenor Coleman Hawkins; and with the highly influential modern saxophonist John Coltrane (a unique meeting that was highlighted by a classic version of "In a Sentimental Mood"). In addition, the Duke Ellington and Count Basie orchestras

were combined for one memorable LP and Ellington's ensemble occasionally toured with Ella Fitzgerald.

There was plenty of new material written during these years. Ellington collaborated with Billy Strayhorn on "Such Sweet Thunder" (a work dedicated to William Shakespeare), "The Girl's Suite," "The Perfume Suite," "The Queen's Suite," a jazz version of Tchaikovsky's "Nutcracker Suite," "Suite Thursday" (based loosely on John Steinbeck's novel *Sweet Thursday*), and a shortened version of "Black, Brown, and Beige" that featured gospel singer Mahalia Jackson. After the good reviews for *Anatomy of a Murder*, Duke was given the opportunity to write the music for 1961's *Paris Blues* (a Paul

Between the mid-1950s and the late 1960s, Duke Ellington and his orchestra occasionally toured with the First Lady of Song, Ella Fitzgerald. She recorded *Ella Fitzgerald Sings the Duke Ellington Songbook* in 1957 with backing from Duke's big band.

LEFT: Ellington was an occasional guest on *The Ed Sullivan Show* in the 1950s and '60s. Although he was usually expected to play concise versions of his veteran hits rather than his lengthier newer material, the appearances helped keep Ellington's name before the general public. **ABOVE:** Shortly after they recorded their only two joint albums, Ellington and Louis Armstrong reprised a couple of the performances on *The Ed Sullivan Show* in 1961.

Newman–Sidney Poitier film that had Louis Armstrong as a supporting star), 1966's *Assault on a Queen*, and 1969's *Change of Mind*. In addition, he and Strayhorn wrote the music for a 1963 civil rights play titled *My People*.

Even an album on which the Duke Ellington orchestra played songs from the movie *Mary Poppins* came off well. No matter what the material (two albums found the band playing then-current pop hits, including "I Want to Hold Your Hand" and "Blowin' in the Wind"), Duke found a way for all of the music to come out fresh and sounding as if it were composed for his band.

Despite the passing years, the personnel of the Ellington orchestra stayed surprisingly stable. Jimmy Woode had become Duke's bassist in 1955 and was succeeded by Aaron Bell in 1960; Booty Wood took over the plunger trombone spot in 1959 when Quentin Jackson departed; the rambunctious trombonist Buster Cooper was a strong replacement for Britt Woodman;

ABOVE: Cootie Williams' return in 1962 was a happy event for Duke Ellington fans. For a short time, both Williams and his successor Ray Nance shared the spotlight, but Nance felt overshadowed and departed in 1963. Cootie, on the other hand, was with the Duke Ellington orchestra until the end of 1974, staying on even after Duke's death. RIGHT: Johnny Hodges' return to Duke Ellington's orchestra in 1955 marked the beginning of Duke's renaissance. For the next fifteen years, Hodges' ballads and blues solos were highlights of every Ellington performance. His sudden death in 1970 left a hole that would never be filled.

and in 1960, Lawrence Brown returned to the band. When Shorty Baker, Clark Terry, and Willie Cook all left Ellington in the early 1960s, the trumpet section simply shrank a bit. Bill Berry took over one spot for a time and then, in 1962, Cootie Williams ended his twenty-two-year "vacation" from the Ellington orchestra (after having been a star soloist for eleven years) to return for the final twelve. The saxophone section remained unchanged for a record nineteen years, from 1950 to 1968.

Ray Nance left in 1963, and there would be other changes in personnel as the members of the Ellington band grew older, but it was not until 1967, with the passing of Billy Strayhorn, that age truly began to be a factor. Strayhorn's untimely death from cancer (he was only fifty-one) served as a violent reminder to Duke that time was no longer on his side. Ellington's orchestra recorded a brilliant posthumous tribute to Strayhorn (...*And His Mother Called Him Bill*) that featured some of the composer's finest songs, and Duke, who in 1965 recorded his first Sacred Concert (he became increasingly religious in later years), would complete two more such tributes in the years to come. His band traveled even more extensively than it had previously, including well-documented visits to Europe (both western and eastern), South America, Mexico, and Asia, reflected in such albums as *Far East Suite*, *Latin American Suite*, and *Afro-Eurasian Eclipse*. Ellington was showered with honors, yet he never won the Pulitzer Prize. He was nominated in the mid-1960s but then turned down—because he was a jazz rather than classical composer—in a controversial move that resulted in some board members resigning in protest.

ABOVE: Two of Duke Ellington's favorite people share a story in the mid 1960s: Billy Strayhorn and Willie "The Lion" Smith. **OPPOSITE:** After his unexpected success at the 1956 Newport Jazz Festival, Duke Ellington was always happy to play Newport. He would be a fixture at that summer festival for most of the next fifteen years.

LEFT: Until just a few weeks before his death from cancer in 1967, Billy Strayhorn continued writing new material, both solo and in collaboration with Ellington. His last composition, "Blood Count," became a classic, and Ellington's first recording after Strayhorn's passing was a moving tribute to his fallen comrade called ...*And His Mother Called Him Bill.* **ABOVE:** Johnny Hodges could always be relied upon to perform memorable music during his features with Duke Ellington, whether it was "Things Ain't What They Used to Be," "Black Butterfly," "Come Sunday," or "Passion Flower."

Jimmy Hamilton ended his twenty-five years with the band in 1968; altoist-flutist Norris Turney and tenor saxo-phonist Harold Ashby soon expanded the saxophone section to six. In 1969, when Duke Ellington celebrated his seventi-eth birthday, his big band could still be considered in its prime, forty-two years after its debut at the Cotton Club. Duke's legacy was celebrated at a tribute concert at the White House and on a two-record set document-ing a concert in England. Mercer Ellington had worked with his father off and on in different capacities for decades; he now had a permanent position in the trumpet section, and he helped run the band. An elder statesman, Duke Ellington was still up-to-date in his wardrobe, his stage personality, and his music.

During these years, pianist Billy Taylor founded and ran Jazzmobile, a series of free out-door concerts that featured jazz musicians play-ing in the streets of Harlem. He remembers this about the time Duke Ellington appeared: "It was August or September 1970. We never thought we'd be able to get Duke for Jazzmobile because, after all, our stage only had room for maybe eight musicians, and it was an outside event that took place in the streets. A woman from the area where we held the concerts told me that she lived in the apartment where he used to live and that I should mention that to him if it would help. Since the people really loved him, I asked Duke, and to my surprise he not only agreed to come play but to

A world traveler for decades by the late 1960s, Ellington even had a couple of opportunities to play in the then Soviet Union and in India. No matter what the spoken language was, his music always communicated.

bring his own orchestra. It was a hot day, so he was sitting in his air-conditioned limo while the band set up. The same woman mentioned that she had air conditioning and asked if he'd like to visit the apartment. Duke was enthusiastic about visiting his former home and, although the woman was just an ordinary housewife, he charmed her for a half-hour. The orchestra played for two hours and the audience was dancing the whole time. At one point Duke thought about stopping but then he spotted a girl dancing on a fire escape and he was inspired to keep on playing. It was a really special day."

Duke Ellington receives an award from Billy Taylor just before playing Jazzmobile in New York in the autumn of 1970.

LEFT: Ellington may have expressed his pride in his race more quietly than some civil rights activists would have liked, but his work and his life spoke for themselves. His talent and elegant bearing won him worldwide recognition and acclaim that paved the way for future generations of African-American artists.

ABOVE: One of Ellington's most famous alumni, tenor great Ben Webster, was forever linked with Duke, even though he was only a full-fledged member of the orchestra for four years, from 1939 to 1943. Webster, who moved permanently to Europe in the mid-1960s, rejoined Ellington for short periods on several occasions during the next three decades, including guesting during several of Duke's European tours.

ABOVE: Duke Ellington's seventieth birthday was celebrated with a lavish black-tie musical party at the White House on April 29, 1969. President Richard Nixon presented the Presidential Medal of Freedom to Ellington during the event, which was widely endorsed by Democrats and Republicans alike. **OPPOSITE:** During his later years, Duke Ellington's three Sacred Concerts were among his most personally cherished projects. Utilizing a choir, guest soloists, dancers, and singers, plus his big band, Ellington created haunting, intriguing music that expressed his deeply felt spirituality.

Inevitably, the end neared. Johnny Hodges passed away in 1970, Lawrence Brown retired, and by 1971 Cat Anderson had left. Ellington, who continued writing long works such as "New Orleans Suite" and "Toga Brava Suite," was able to welcome a few newer voices to his band (most notably trumpeters Barry Lee Hall and Money Johnson and altoist Harold Minerve) and he recorded some notable small-group combo dates during 1972–73 (including a quartet set with guitarist Joe Pass). But his voice was becoming raspy due to illness and his orchestra was starting to decline musically.

Duke Ellington's last recording took place in England on December 1, 1973. Other than the saxophone section, the orchestra was filled mostly with lesser-known names, and Duke's piano was featured more prominently than usual. Ellington showed throughout that he had not lost his spirit, concluding with the touching piano solo "Meditation."

LEFT: Ellington often said, "I was born 1956 at the Newport festival." **ABOVE:** Paul Gonsalves, whose twenty-seven-chorus marathon solo bridging "Diminuendo in Blue" and "Crescendo in Blue" at the 1956 Newport Jazz Festival launched Duke Ellington's "comeback," was one of Duke's key soloists in the 1960s and early '70s. Gonsalves' harmonically advanced style and ability to play lengthy solos compensated for his occasional unreliability, and he was with Duke until the day he died, just ten days before Ellington's own demise.

Ellington's health gradually declined during the next few months, although he continued appearing with his band into March 1974. During his last weeks he completed the writing for a comic opera, *Queenie Pie*, and added some final details to his ballet suite "The Three Black Kings." On his seventy-fifth birthday, several concerts were performed in his honor and a full issue of *Down Beat* was filled with praise from the top players in the jazz world.

On May 24, 1974, Duke Ellington passed away from lung cancer at the age of seventy-five. His orchestra was taken over by Mercer Ellington and for a time continued, featuring Harry Carney (who died later in the year) and Cootie Williams. It eventually became just a part-time affair, and remained so until Mercer's death on February 8, 1996.

Since its leader's passing, the Duke Ellington orchestra's previously unreleased recordings have been issued on a regular basis, almost as if he were still alive, and in

OPPOSITE: Ellington remained active until the end of his life, completing suites and a ballet while in a hospital room as he turned seventy-five. He had no plans to ever retire and he remained innovative until the very end. **ABOVE:** There will never be another Duke Ellington, just like no replacement has ever come along for Bach, Mozart, Beethoven, Louis Armstrong, or Charlie Parker. But fortunately the amount of unreleased "new" music from Ellington that is waiting to see the light of day seems to be endless.

recent years most of his tremendous number of recordings have been reissued on compact disc. Whether in the chord voicings of most modern jazz pianists, the arranging techniques of today's composers, the hundreds of his songs and suites that are still being recorded, or the adventurous spirit demonstrated on the part of all creative jazz musicians, Duke Ellington's legacy lives on.

THE LEGACY OF DUKE ELLINGTON

EPILOGUE

Ellington, who never lost his enthusiasm for music or for his band, cheers on Paul Gonsalves in the late 1960s.

D r. Billy Taylor has this to say about Duke Ellington: "I think Duke may have been the finest American composer of any genre. The music he wrote was comparable to Debussy and Ravel and yet was different, drawing influences from many different areas and turning them into jazz. People are constantly discovering how much of a master he was, and the amount of originality that went into writing an unusual song such as 'Sophisticated Lady.'"

In the April 1, 1925, issue of *Variety,* a review of the Kentucky Club Show stated in part: "Probably the 'hottest' band this side of the equator is the dance feature at this basement cabaret formerly known as the Hollywood. It is Duke Ellington's Washingtonians, a colored combo that plays 'blues' as nobody can. The jazz boys who drop in at the place, which runs well into the morning and past dawn, take much delight in sitting around and drinking in their indigo modulations." Even at that early stage, Duke Ellington stood apart from the crowd.

ABOVE, LEFT: 1949's *Symphony in Swing* was one of Duke Ellington's better film shorts. Five songs were performed, highlighted by "Take the 'A' Train," "On a Turquoise Cloud" (with singer Kay Davis), and an adventurous rendition of "Frankie and Johnny." **ABOVE, RIGHT:** *Salute to Duke Ellington,* a fifteen-minute-long film made in 1950, was the last short film that Duke made.

There was just something about his music and the aura that surrounded him that made him unique.

Ellington's legacy reaches beyond music: his prodigious talent and his pride in his race paved the way for African-American musicians and artists for generations to come. The Hollywood stereotype of a jazz player in the 1920s was unreliable, spoke in instantly dated jive talk, and was a constant partygoer who showed up late and never seemed to get anything done despite his intuitive talents. While white musicians were seen as lovable social outcasts, black musicians were portrayed as being only a step above the "happy savages" of Africa, blessed with talent but otherwise inferior. But almost from the start, Duke Ellington's obvious genius and his dignified manner allowed him to reach levels of public acceptance and respect almost unheard-of for people of his race during the Jim Crow years. He never "Uncle Tommed" in films, which is why, decades later, his appearances on screen seem timeless and very human—unlike those of many of his contemporaries.

As Duke Ellington advanced into his sixties, he stayed aware of current musical trends, yet continued writing and playing in a timeless style. He also never missed an opportunity to say to an audience, "I love you madly."

In the 1960s, some civil rights activists felt that Ellington should be taking to the streets and joining their demonstrations. Others were quick to point out, however, that Ellington had been fighting for equality in subtler ways for decades, from using the word "black" with pride since the mid-1920s (including in the title of such songs as "Black Beauty," "Black and Tan Fantasy," the "Black, Brown, and Beige" suite, and "Black Butterfly") to his 1941 play *Jump for Joy*. That he was able to overcome or at least appear to ignore the petty and often dangerous racism of his times without giving in to it (or letting it slow down his work) was quite admirable. Never mind that Ellington could not eat in many restaurants or sleep in quite a few hotel rooms on the road because of the color of his skin. Through his brilliance, likable personality, and good humor, he was able to transcend

Duke Ellington's talent and charm earned him respect and admiration wherever he went. As President Nixon said at Ellington's seventieth birthday celebration at the White House, "In the royalty of American music, no man swings more or stands higher than the Duke."

many of the problems of the times, thereby helping to break down barriers and make things a little easier for future generations.

Duke Ellington's legacy can be felt throughout jazz and popular music in countless ways. Ellington did not invent jazz or swing, but his ideas sped up the music's evolution. In the late 1920s, he was one of the very first arranger-composers to write specifically for the strengths and around the weaknesses of his sidemen. Most other bands of the time used more generic charts (known as "stocks") that could be utilized by nearly any jazz or dance orchestra. In the early years of the Depression, long after their key arranger, Don Redman, had left to work elsewhere, even Fletcher Henderson's orchestra often used stocks, leaving it up to the soloists to give the music a personality of its own that hopefully would differ from the interpretations of other bands using the same arrangements. However, Duke Ellington never used these functional but predictable charts; why should he when he could quickly rewrite, reinvent, and uplift any song? During the swing era, any orchestra that sought to succeed had to have its own sound rather than relying too much on freelance arrangers. Duke knew that a decade earlier.

Early on, some other bands tried their best to sound like Ellington's. In 1933, Jack Hylton's orchestra in England recorded *Ellingtonia*, a medley of some of Duke's then-recent recordings ("Black and Tan Fantasy," "It Don't Mean a Thing," "Mood Indigo," and "Bugle Call Rag") that found Hylton's band doing a very close re-creation of Ellington's sound of the time. As impressive as that effort still is, it was clearly a departure for Hylton that was successful due to his arranger's ability to transcribe from Duke's records and his sidemen's admiration for Ellington's soloists.

Duke Ellington's mysterious genius for getting unique sounds from his orchestra can be summed up by this famous quote from pianist-arranger André Previn, which first appeared in Nat Shapiro and Nat Hentoff's book *The Jazz Makers:* "Stan Kenton can stand in front of a thousand fiddles and a thousand brass and make a dramatic gesture and every studio arranger can nod his head and say, 'Oh, yes, that's done like this.' But Duke merely lifts his finger, three horns make a sound, and I don't know what it is!"

That Ellington broke the rules rather than merely following them, that his ensemble sounded unlike anyone else's, and that his recordings from as far back as 1927 still sound fresh and alive today means that he set the

Ellington constantly tinkered with his compositions, reworking and rerecording pieces to suit the ever-changing lineup of his orchestra and his own mercurial artistic sensibility.

standard for future jazz musicians. The point in jazz is not to sound like everyone else but instead to create one's own distinctive world of musical ideas, sounds, and repertoire. The music should not be only of the time (as in pop music) but for all time.

It is true that Duke Ellington's compositions sounded best when performed by his orchestra, and that many of his sidemen's post-Ellington careers were anti-climactic. Duke knew his player's capabilities so well that they rarely sounded as consistent outside of his universe. During his twenty-one-year "vacation" between lengthy stints with Ellington, Cootie Williams spent a fruitful year with Benny Goodman's orchestra and then led his own big band. Although the trumpeter worked steadily for a few years and featured some notable sidemen (including pianist Bud Powell, altoist-singer Eddie "Cleanhead" Vinson, and the honking tenor of Willis "Gator" Jackson), the second half of Williams' solo career was quite uneventful and mostly spent in obscurity, out of the spotlight. His style was considered old-fashioned, at least until it was revived after his return to Duke.

An all-star gathering in the mid-1940s, with vibraphonist Red Norvo, bassist John Kirby, vibraphonist Lionel Hampton, Ellington, and trumpeter-vocalist Louis Armstrong. Although they recorded one song together in 1946, Duke and Satchmo did not meet up on records until 1961, when Ellington played piano with Armstrong's All-Stars—which included Ellington's former clarinetist Barney Bigard—on an extended set of Duke's compositions.

Cootie Williams worked with Ellington for twenty-three years. Here, Cootie and Duke take a cigarette break.

Clarinetist Barney Bigard mostly played New Orleans jazz and dixieland after leaving Ellington in 1942, including a couple of stints with Louis Armstrong's All-Stars, but he never sounded all that challenged by the material he performed after his Duke years ended. Even altoist Johnny Hodges, among the most popular of Ellington's players, who had a hit with "Castle Rock" (which actually featured tenorman Al Sears) shortly after leaving Duke in 1951, only stayed away for four years. Most of his projects away from the composer ended up sounding like a small-group

Ellington session anyway. And such major players as Bubber Miley, Ray Nance, and Jimmy Hamilton did surprisingly little of significance after leaving Ellington.

A few musicians had very productive post-Ellington careers, particularly Louie Bellson, Ben Webster, and Clark Terry. But it is notable that Bellson was with Ellington for just two years and Webster fewer than four, and yet they were both identified with Duke throughout their long careers.

Throughout its unprecedented forty-nine-year run (1925–1974), the Duke Ellington orchestra was one of the few long-term jazz institutions. Of the other key big bands, Benny Goodman's longest-running orchestra had only seven years together (1934–1941) before poor health caused a temporary breakup. Artie Shaw started and broke up bands every couple of years, and Glenn Miller's civilian orchestra was around for just a little more than four years (1938–1942). Woody Herman traveled with big bands for fifty years but took many brief lay-offs; the same can be said for Stan Kenton, who lasted thirty. Only the Count Basie (1935–1984) and Les Brown (1938–present) orchestras are comparable to Ellington's in longevity. But

ABOVE: Billy Strayhorn consistently inspired Duke Ellington from 1939 until 1967. Strayhorn was originally hired as a lyricist and sometimes filled in on piano, but above all he was Duke's writing collaborator. His arrangements and compositions were sometimes indistinguishable from Ellington's, leading to his being overshadowed through the years, but Duke always knew his value. **OPPOSITE:** Duke Ellington's mighty brass section of the early 1930s: Juan Tizol, Tricky Sam Nanton, and Lawrence Brown on trombones and Cootie Williams, Arthur Whetsol, and Freddy Jenkins on trumpets. All of them were highly original.

Basie had a two-year period (1950–52) during which he was forced to cut back to a combo, while Brown's orchestra spent much of its history operating as an anonymous backup big band for Bob Hope and other commercial acts. Only Duke Ellington was able to keep a creative jazz orchestra together for such a long time, and it is remarkable to think that, artistically at least, the band never had a real "off" period.

The hundredth anniversary of Duke Ellington's birth occurred in 1999, and the many celebrations that surrounded his centennial served as good excuses for many musicians to explore Duke's compositions, both his three-minute miniatures and his more extended works. But one cannot really say that the centennial started a rediscovery or renaissance of Duke Ellington's music (as the 1974 film *The Sting* did for Scott Joplin's compositions); since the late 1920s, musicians have been very much aware of the richness of his songs. Duke's music has been explored by Dixieland bands, bop combos, and swing groups—Count Basie's orchestra has had "In a Mellotone" in their books for decades. Avant-garde tenor saxophonist Archie Shepp has often performed Duke pieces, and in 1981 the innovative pianist Ran Blake recorded a full album of Ellington and Strayhorn numbers called *Duke Dreams*. Ella Fitzgerald and Sarah Vaughan are among the many singers, both within and outside of jazz, who have recorded full-length Ellington songbooks. Even fusion groups have recorded Ellington's work: Joe Zawinul's Weather Report once cut a version of "Rockin' in Rhythm."

It seemed as if Duke Ellington was always part of the contemporary American music scene. His orchestra played a constant stream of new music along with his earlier hits whenever they performed. Although the master passed away in 1974, there is no chance that he will be forgotten. The quantity of Ellington's output during half a century of constant writing is enormous, and the consistently high quality of these treasures ensures that his legacy will not dim with time.

"Beyond category" was one of Duke Ellington's favorite sayings, an expression of admiration that he reserved for the artists he respected most. No one deserved this description more than he did.

BIBLIOGRAPHY

Bigard, Barney. *With Louis and the Duke: The Autobiography of a Jazz Clarinetist,* ed. Barry Martyn. New York: Oxford University Press, 1985.

Collier, James Lincoln. *Duke Ellington.* New York: Oxford University Press, 1987.

Dance, Stanley. *The World of Duke Ellington.* New York: Da Capo, 1970.

Ellington, Duke. *Music Is My Mistress.* New York: Doubleday, 1973.

Ellington, Mercer, with Stanley Dance. *Duke Ellington in Person: An Intimate Memoir.* Boston: Houghton Mifflin, 1978, 1988.

Gammond, Peter, ed. *Duke Ellington: His Life and Music.* Foreword by Hughes Panassié. New York: Da Capo, 1977.

George, Don. *Sweet Man: The Real Duke Ellington.* New York: G.P. Putnam's Sons, 1981.

Hajdu, David. *Lush Life.* New York: Farrar, Straus & Giroux, 1996.

Hasse, John Edward. *Beyond Category: The Life and Genius of Duke Ellington.* New York: Simon and Schuster, 1993.

Jewell, Derek. *Duke: A Portrait of Duke Ellington.* New York: W.W. Norton, 1977.

Shapiro, Nat and Nat Hentoff, eds. *The Jazz Makers: Essays on the Greats of Jazz.* New York: Da Capo Press, 1979.

Stewart, Rex. *Boy Meets Horn*, ed. Claire P. Gordon. Ann Arbor: University of Michigan Press, 1991.

Stratemann, Klaus. *Ellington Day by Day and Film by Film.* Copenhagen: JazzMedia, 1992.

Timner, W. E., comp. *Ellingtonia: The Recorded Music of Duke Ellington and His Sidemen.* London: Institute of Jazz Studies and Scarecrow Press, 1996.

Tucker, Mark. *Ellington: The Early Years.* Urbana: University of Illinois Press, 1991.

———, ed. *The Duke Ellington Reader.* New York: Oxford University Press, 1993.

Ulanov, Barry. *Duke Ellington.* New York: Da Capo Press, 1975.

RECOMMENDED LISTENING

There are literally hundreds of Duke Ellington recordings currently available. Here are some of the most essential and historic.

Birth of A Band—Hot 'N' Sweet 5104 (1924–26) Duke Ellington's earliest recordings are on this intriguing CD, which captures his orchestra gradually finding its own sound after some primitive false starts. In addition to some numbers by the big band, there are selections in which pianist Ellington backs a variety of singers.

The Complete Brunswick and Vocalion Recordings—Decca GRD-3-640 (1926–31) This three-CD set starts with the very first session (November 29, 1926) on which the Ellington orchestra sounds distinctive (resulting in "East St. Louis Toodle-oo" and "Birmingham Breakdown") and continues through its Cotton Club years. The sixty-seven performances contain more than their share of classic gems and the reissue complements (but does not duplicate) the Columbia and Bluebird reissues.

The Okeh Ellington—Columbia 46177 (1927–30) Duke Ellington's Okeh records of the late 1920s were not as celebrated as his sides for Victor but were often their equals. The fifty selections (which unfortunately do not include any of the alternate takes) are highlighted by "East St. Louis Toodle-oo," "Black and Tan Fantasy," "The Mooche," "Mood Indigo," and Ellington's first two solo piano recordings.

Early Ellington—Bluebird 6852 (1927–34); *Jungle Nights in Harlem*—Bluebird 2497 (1927–32); *Jubilee Stomp*—Bluebird 66038 (1928–34) While Decca and Columbia have reissued all of their early Duke Ellington recordings on CD, RCA (in its Bluebird series) has thus far adapted a piecemeal approach, coming out with these three discs that cover the overlapping period without duplicating each other or being very complete. *Early Ellington*, which includes "Black and Tan Fantasy," "Creole Love Call," "Black Beauty," "Mood Indigo," and the remarkable "Daybreak Express," gets the edge, but RCA is long overdue to make all of their early Duke performances available in a more coherent fashion. These will do in the meantime.

Solos, Duets, and Trios—Bluebird 2178 (1932–67) Since Duke Ellington tends to be underrated as a pianist (due to his many other talents), this CD is valuable because it features the genius in several different settings. Ellington plays duets with Billy Strayhorn, is heard taking piano solos during three different decades, teams up with pianist Earl "Fatha" Hines, leads a trio, and is in a supportive role on four duets (plus five alternate takes) with the brilliant bassist Jimmie Blanton.

Small Groups, Vol. 1—Columbia/Legacy C2K 46995 (1934–38) To keep his sidemen happy—and to try out new compositions—Duke Ellington sponsored and participated in a series of small group dates "led" by some of his top players. On this two-CD set (which has forty-five selections but no alternate takes), cornetist Rex Stewart, clarinetist Barney Bigard, trumpeter

Cootie Williams, and altoist Johnny Hodges get top billing. There are many hot stomps plus early versions of "Caravan," "Stompy Jones," and "Echoes of Harlem," which were soon to become standards in Ellington's repertoire.

Small Groups, Vol. 2—Columbia/Legacy C2K 48835 (1938–39) Forty-three more performances from combo sessions headed by Duke Ellington's sidemen are reissued on this two-CD set. Johnny Hodges, Cootie Williams, and Rex Stewart are the main stars and, along with plenty of heated obscurities, such tunes as "Jeep's Blues," "Pyramid," "Prelude to a Kiss," and "The Jeep Is Jumping" are heard in their first recordings.

In Boston 1939–1940—Jazz Unlimited 2022 (1939–40) The Duke Ellington orchestra is featured on a pair of rare radio broadcasts on this disc, playing near the peak of its powers. Bassist Jimmie Blanton is prominent, as are seven major horn soloists and the pianist-leader, performing their repertoire of the period in consistently inspired fashion. Ivie Anderson and Herb Jeffries contribute a few vocals.

The Blanton/Webster Band—Bluebird 5659 (1939–42) This brilliant three-CD set captures the Duke Ellington orchestra during one of its greatest periods. The sixty-six recordings (the orchestra's entire output for Victor from a three-year period) include dozens of classics such as "Concerto for Cootie," "Cottontail," "Harlem Airshaft," "All Too Soon," "In a Mellotone," "Take the 'A' Train," "I Got It Bad," "Rocks in My Bed," "Chelsea Bridge," "Perdido," and "The 'C' Jam Blues." The Ellington big band had ten distinctive and consistently inspired soloists, Jimmie Blanton and Ben Webster being the ensemble's latest additions.

The Great Ellington Units—Bluebird 6751 (1940–41) After switching from Columbia to Victor, Duke

Ellington continued sponsoring small-group dates headed by his sidemen. On this single CD the debuts of "Things Ain't What They Used to Be," "Passion Flower," and "The 'C' Jam Blues" are among the high points. Johnny Hodges, Rex Stewart, and Barney Bigard are the leaders but one can feel Ellington's guiding hand throughout.

Fargo, ND—Vintage Jazz Classics 1019/20 (1940) It was pure luck that engineer Jack Towers, who was then a young Ellington fan, captured Duke's orchestra on a very good night, playing what would otherwise have been a long-forgotten gig in Fargo, North Dakota. This double CD has all of the music that Towers recorded during what was cornetist Ray Nance's first performance with the band; among the other stars are Ben Webster (superb on "Stardust"), Rex Stewart, Tricky Sam Nanton, Johnny Hodges, and Jimmie Blanton.

The Carnegie Hall Concerts (January 1943)—Prestige 34004 (1943) Duke Ellington's first Carnegie Hall concert, released in full on this two-CD set, is highlighted by the debut of his monumental suite "Black, Brown, and Beige," along with many superior miniatures that include both older and more recent compositions.

Black, Brown, and Beige—Bluebird 6641 (1944–46) Although Ellington's band was undergoing more turnover during the mid-1940s than it had previously, the quality of its music remained very high. This three-CD set has the studio version (actually excerpts) of "Black, Brown, and Beige," many newly arranged versions of older Duke classics, and some excellent new pieces.

The Carnegie Hall Concerts (December 1947)—Prestige 24075 (1947) Prestige has reissued music from four of Duke Ellington's Carnegie Hall concerts (including sets from 1944 and 1946). This

two-CD release is second in quality only to the 1943 one. It is highlighted by a superior version of the "Liberian Suite" (which has many fine solos including contributions from Tyree Glenn on vibes and Ray Nance on violin), a Johnny Hodges medley, the nearly atonal "Clothed Woman," a trumpet battle on "Blue Skies," and some stomping spots for Al Sears' tenor.

The Carnegie Hall Concerts (November 1948)—Vintage Jazz Classics 1024/25 (1948) Due to a recording strike by the Musicians Union, Duke Ellington's orchestra was barely documented in 1948, a transitional year. However, the sixth and final in his series of acclaimed Carnegie Hall concerts was taped and this two-CD set shows that there was never any real decline in Duke's music. Ben Webster was temporarily back in the band and other key soloists heard from are Johnny Hodges, Al Sears, clarinetist Jimmy Hamilton, Ray Nance, and trumpeter Shorty Baker. "The Tattooed Bride" was premiered, and there are some surprising revivals of older compositions, plus one of the few Ellington performances of Billy Strayhorn's "Lush Life."

Uptown—Columbia 40836 (1951–52) The best all-around recording from Duke Ellington's so-called "off" period (when Johnny Hodges was out leading his own band), this set has many classic moments. Betty Roché delivers a famous bebop vocal on "Take the 'A' Train,' "The Mooche" puts the focus on the contrasting clarinet styles of Russell Procope and Jimmy Hamilton, "Perdido" features trumpeter Clark Terry, Louie Bellson's drum solo on "Skin Deep" was famous, and the two-part "Controversial Suite" contrasts New Orleans jazz with futuristic music.

Piano Reflections—Capitol 92863 (1953) This set is a special treat, for it puts the spotlight on

Duke Ellington as a pianist playing with a trio. Throughout the program, Ellington sounds quite modern (particularly rhythmically and in his chord voicings) and shows that he was one of the few pianists to effectively evolve from stride to post-bop.

Ellington at Newport—Columbia 40587 (1956) This recording documents a historic event, Duke Ellington's "comeback" concert. At the 1956 Newport Jazz Festival his orchestra performed the inventive if overlooked "Newport Jazz Festival Suite" and a Johnny Hodges feature ("Jeep's Blues"). However, it was the band's rendition of "Diminuendo" and "Crescendo in Blue" that caused a sensation, highlighted by Paul Gonsalves' hard-swinging twenty-seven-chorus tenor solo. One can hear the place gradually going wild!

Live at the Blue Note—Roulette 72438 28637 (1958) The Blue Note club in Chicago was one of Duke Ellington's favorite venues. This two-CD set brings back a full night by the Ellington band. The three nearly complete sets include old favorites, newer material, Billy Strayhorn sitting in on his "Take the 'A' Train," a few selections from the recent *Anatomy of a Murder* soundtrack, a couple of numbers where both Ellington and Strayhorn are on piano, and an eleven-minute version of "Mood Indigo."

Three Suites—Columbia 46825 (1960) Three of Duke Ellington's better extended works from the era are included on this reissue: his delightful reworking of Tchaikovsky's "Nutcracker Suite," Grieg's "Peer Gynt Suites," and a tribute to John Steinbeck, "Suite Thursday."

First Time! The Count Meets the Duke—Columbia 8515 (1961) This is a crazy concept that worked. The entire big bands of Duke Ellington and Count Basie were combined to make a super

orchestra that included the leaders on twin pianos! The mutual respect of the two bandleaders, some inventive planning, and many inspired arrangements resulted in remarkable music that is somehow uncrowded: "Segue in 'C,'" "Until I Met You," "Battle Royal," and "Jumpin' at the Woodside" are highlights.

Money Jungle—Blue Note 46398 (1962) Duke Ellington was a remarkably modern pianist for one who came to artistic maturity in the 1920s. Proof of that is heard throughout this disc, which teams Duke in a trio with bassist Charles Mingus and drummer Max Roach. Although his sidemen were from a much later generation, Ellington sounds like the youngest player of the three.

Duke Ellington and John Coltrane—Impulse 166 (1962) In the early 1960s, Duke Ellington had the opportunity to record with such fellow veterans as Count Basie, Louis Armstrong, and Coleman Hawkins. For this successful recording, Ellington joined the John Coltrane Quartet (sometimes using his own bassist and drummer). Coltrane, one of the giants of the 1960s and 1970s, loved Ellington's music and his rendition of "In a Sentimental Mood" is a classic.

The Great Paris Concert—Atlantic 304 (1963) Nearly forty years after forming his orchestra, Duke Ellington was still at the top of his field. This two-CD release shows what it was like to experience the orchestra at the time. Among the memorable moments are "Rockin' in Rhythm," "Concerto for Cootie," "Jam with Sam," "Suite Thursday," and the "Harlem Suite."

The Far East Suite, Special Mix—Bluebird 66551 (1966) This nine-part suite was arguably Duke Ellington's finest major work of the 1960s. "Isfahan" (a ballad showcase for Johnny Hodges) is the best-known section but most of the other

themes (including "Bluebird of Delhi," and "Ad Lib on Nippon") also stay in one's memory. Jimmy Hamilton and Paul Gonsalves are prominently featured, along with Hodges.

...And His Mother Called Him Bill—Bluebird 6287 (1967) After Billy Strayhorn's death in 1967, the Duke Ellington orchestra recorded a dozen of his compositions. Their interpretations are emotional, passionate, and quite inspired with "Blood Count," "Rain Check," "Lotus Blossom," and "The Intimacy of The Blues" receiving definitive treatments.

70th Birthday Concert—Blue Note 32746 (1969) One of Duke Ellington's last great recordings, this double-CD finds his orchestra mostly remaking his older hits but in fresh new ways. The program serves as a retrospective without merely being nostalgic. "Rockin' in Rhythm" has rarely swung more, Cootie Williams is wonderful on "Take the 'A' Train," organist Wild Bill Davis has a few guest spots, the hits medley really works well, and Cat Anderson has an incredible high-note trumpet chorus on "Satin Doll." Overall, this is the perfect introduction to the magical music of Duke Ellington.

The Afro-Eurasian Eclipse—Original Jazz Classics 345 (1971) An intriguing late-period output from the Duke Ellington orchestra with one number ("Acht o'Clock Rock") even showing off the influence of rock. Other pieces show that Ellington was interested in both African folk music and more advanced areas of jazz, but he always retained his band's personality.

The Duke's Big Four—Pablo 2310-703 (1973) Recorded a little more than a year before Duke Ellington's death, he teams up in a quartet with guitarist Joe Pass, bassist Ray Brown, and drummer Louie Bellson, showing how modern his percussive piano style still was.

FILMOGRAPHY

Black and Tan (1929, short subject). Contains "Black and Tan Fantasy," "Black Beauty," and "Cotton Club Stomp," among others, and showcases the Cotton Club dancers.

Check and Double Check (1930). An Amos 'n' Andy comedy featuring Ellington and the orchestra performing "Old Man Blues."

A Bundle of Blues (1933, short subject). Contains "Stormy Weather" (sung by Ivie Anderson), "Bugle Call Rag," and "Rockin' in Rhythm."

Murder at the Vanities (1934). Includes "Ebony Rhapsody" and a scene of an angry conductor machine-gunning the Ellington orchestra for playing a jazzy version of Liszt's "Hungarian Rhapsody."

Belle of the Nineties (1934). Features Mae West performing four non-Ellington pop songs accompanied by Ellington's orchestra.

Symphony in Black: A Rhapsody of Negro Life (1934). Ellington composed the score and he and his orchestra star in this short film on African-American life.

The Hit Parade (1937). Features Ivie Anderson and the orchestra performing "It Don't Mean a Thing (If It Ain't Got That Swing)."

Cabin in the Sky (1942). This landmark film has an all-black cast and features Ellington performing "Goin' Up" and "Things Ain't What They Used to Be."

Reveille with Beverly (1942). Filled with appearances by swing bands and pop singers of the day, this film includes Ellington's orchestra, featuring Betty Roché and Ray Nance, performing "Take the 'A' Train."

Date with Duke (1947). This short-subject cartoon contains excerpts from "The Perfume Suite."

Symphony in Swing (1949, short subject). Five songs are performed, including "On a Turquois Cloud," which features Kay Davis, and an adventerous rendition of "Frankie and Johnny."

The Asphalt Jungle (1950). Ellington composed the soundtrack.

Anatomy of a Murder (1959). Ellington composed the score, performs it with his orchestra, and has a brief scene with star Jimmy Stewart.

Paris Blues (1961). Ellington composed the score.

Duke Ellington in Europe (performance video, 1963–64). Shot in Stockholm and London, this includes "Dancers in Love," "The Blues," and "Tutti for Cootie."

Assault on a Queen (1966). Ellington composed the soundtrack.

On the Road with Duke Ellington (video, 1967). Made originally for NBC's *Bell Telephone Hour*, this documentary features Ellington performing and discussing his music and his collaboration with Billy Strayhorn.

Change of Mind (1969). Ellington composed the soundtrack.

Memories of the Duke (1980). This documentary, shot mainly in Mexico, features "Mexican Suite," "Black and Tan Fantasy," "Satin Doll," and others.

Sophisticated Ladies (video, 1982). This Broadway revue, based on Duke Ellington's songs, was arranged and conducted by Mercer Ellington.

The Sacred Music of Duke Ellington (video, 1982). Filmed in London, this concert includes performances by Adelaide Hall, Phillis Hyman, and Tony Bennett.

PHOTO CREDITS

Archive Photos: p. 58; Frank Driggs Collection: pp. 62, 76; Metronome Collection: pp. 13, 22 right, 23, 31 left, 32, 36 left, 37, 54–55, 75 right, 80

Ray Avery's Jazz Archive: pp. 31 right, 36 right, 38–39, 45 left, 71, 78–79, 82–83, 90, 93 right, 101 right, 104–105, 112

Corbis/Bettmann Archives: p. 86 right; Penguin: pp. 10, 48; John Springer: p. 29; Underwood & Underwood: pp. 6–7, 92–93; UPI: pp. 15 top, 15 bottom, 34, 56–57, 68–69, 98

Courtesy of Creative Music Publicity: p. 95

Frank Driggs Collection: 11, 18–19, 20, 21 left, 24–25, 25 right, 26–27, 28, 30, 35, 40–41, 41 right, 42–43, 44, 45 right, 46, 47, 49 left, 49 right, 50–51, 51 right, 52 left, 52 right, 53, 59, 60, 61, 63, 64, 65 right, 66, 67, 70 right, 73, 74, 79 top right, 81, 86 left, 87 right

National Museum of American History: pp. 12, 16, 33, 54–55, 77, 85, 87 left, 94, 99, 100–101, 107, 109, 115

Retna/©William Gottlieb: p. 70 left

Retna/©David Redfern: p. 84, 96–97, 102, 110, 111

Schomburg Center for Research in Black Culture/New York Public Library: pp. 5, 14, 21 right, 22 left, 108, 113

Separate Cinema: p. 38 left, 65 left, 75 left, 106 left, 106 right

©Lee Tanner: pp. 2, 17, 72, 79 bottom right, 88 left, 88–89, 91, 96, 103

©Carol Weinberg: p. 9

INDEX